T0384219

Leaner Six Sigma

Leaner Six Sigma

Making Lean Six Sigma Easier and Adaptable to Current Workplaces

Terra Vanzant Stern, PhD

Routledge
Taylor & Francis Group
A PRODUCTIVITY PRESS BOOK

First edition published in 2019
by Routledge/Productivity Press
52 Vanderbilt Avenue, 11th Floor New York, NY 10017
2 Park Square, Milton Park, Abingdon, Oxon OX14 4RN, UK

© 2019 by Terra Vanzant Stern, PhD
Routledge/Productivity Press is an imprint of Taylor & Francis Group, an Informa business

No claim to original U.S. Government works

Printed on acid-free paper

International Standard Book Number-13: 978-1-138-38792-8 (Hardback)
978-0-429-42596-7 (eBook)

Visit the Taylor & Francis Web site at
http://www.taylorandfrancis.com

and the CRC Press Web site at
http://www.crcpress.com

Dedication

To all the delightful clients and students who supported

my effort to make Lean Six Sigma, even Leaner!

Contents

SECTION I   The Basics—Making Things Better, Faster or More Cost Effective

SECTION II   The DMAIC Model

SECTION III   Standards

Preface

Kiichiro Toyoda, founder of the Toyota Motor Corporation, believed in a philosophy that I embrace: "The ideal conditions for making things are created when machines, facilities and people work together to add value without generating any waste."

In the beginning of my career I played a role in executive-level Human Resources (HR). I was often told the people, at our company, were broken. At that time, there was not an understanding or appreciation about how employees, equipment, policies and facilities worked together to form processes. I facilitated many meetings that focused on team difficulties, failed expectations of employees, leadership problems and the lack of employee motivation. My professional peers held entire conferences on how to manage conflict in the workplace, how to document employee issues and how to gracefully terminate positions.

I always had an underlying suspicion that most employees wanted to do a good job. That no one was actually "broken." We all want the same things out of work. These include, but are not limited to, a sense of accomplishment, a feeling of belonging and a desire to contribute something bigger than ourselves. The money and the benefits are prime in our employment pursuits, but once that is secured, we move to higher ground.

Later, I worked for a CEO who did not totally grasp what the HR Department did. He saw us more as a nuisance than a helpmate. He started assigning me projects that had nothing to do with HR even though my title said I was a Senior Director of that department. This turned out to be my greatest career experience prior to joining my current company SSD Global Solutions.

We were in the process of going public and somehow I inherited a lot of additional responsibilities. Anything that was not income producing became part of my universe. As various department heads quit, I was given the "interim" ownership. In less than 6 months, I was handling the project management office, the International Standards department, the risk management group and what remained of the Six Sigma department.

It occurred to me that many of my new roles had to do with managing necessary overhead. Since *profit was king* in the organization and these departments "spent" money, it would be difficult to document my value.

It did not help that I knew nothing about what these departments did on a daily basis. I facilitated a number of focus groups in an effort to understand the core responsibilities of each group. This led to more meetings about team difficulties, failed expectations of employees, leadership problems and lack of employee motivation. I was getting nowhere.

I read constantly in an effort to learn what was needed to make each unit successful. And I started repeating the words of H. James Harrington who claimed, "Measurement is the first step that leads to control and eventually to improvement. If you can't measure something you can't understand it. If you can't understand it, you can't control it. If you can't control it, you can't improve it." It was almost like a mantra.

My first attempt at finding synergy between all the departments led me to project management. The more I learned about our project management group, the more I realized we were all managing projects. Simply applying some of the core concepts of project management to my business life made everything easier. Identifying and discussing specific projects for each department also shortened my learning curve.

Even my own department, HR, began to benefit. We started looking at HR activities as projects instead of tasks. We began to examine our Return-on-Investment (ROI) for our advertising and hiring processes. Next, our training department became a profit center by offering some of our internal programs to surrounding companies. Henry Ford said, "If you always do what you've always done, you'll always get what you've always got."

Once I understood the mission of the departments I acquired I was able to offer training and support. These internal groups were often comprised of only 3–4 students. So, we started inviting and charging people from the community to participate in our training. This not only covered our training expenses and fees but left us with a surplus. This surplus was ultimately used to fund additional professional development efforts. These development efforts morphed into conducting classes in Six Sigma which was a popular offering at the time.

When I first became involved with Six Sigma, my newly discovered project management education was incredibly helpful. Six Sigma is applied to existing processes and work to make these processes better, faster or more cost effective. The realization that Six Sigma had major components that dealt with project management led me to the thought of focusing on the synergy between these two sciences as opposed to the differences.

Probably the major difference I noticed between Project Management and Six Sigma is that in Six Sigma projects, there was an additional component to sustain the project and move toward continuous improvement. Many of my regular projects simply had a beginning and end. In fact, that is somewhat included in the definition of a project. But, Six Sigma, had a continued interest in process improvement.

I started practicing on some of the concepts in the various departments. At first, I noticed that this effort was not highly appreciated among department heads. This seemed puzzling to me since we were showing ROI that had never been documented. Surely my new departments, considered by some as simply necessary waste, would welcome the opportunity to demonstrate and validate their true value.

I rapidly realized that, although the methodology made perfect sense to me, Six Sigma seemed a tedious process to other employees in the company. I read about a company that was using Lean and Six Sigma together. What I liked about the concept of blending Lean with Six Sigma is that Lean appeared to have a better understanding of the people component. Certainly, the Body of Knowledge regarding Six Sigma appreciated the leadership and team factors necessary to make the project work. But, Lean went one step further in understanding the needs of the individuals working on projects.

Balancing the Lean side of Lean Six Sigma with standard Six Sigma also allowed for a movement away from always doing projects using waterfall methodology. Whereas waterfall methodology worked incredibly well on large projects, there were many smaller projects that would benefit from using the DMAIC in a circular fashion. In large projects, it is not uncommon for different departments to handle different facets of the model.

Therefore, it is important that one step is finished before the next step begins. On smaller projects, however, one project manager may be responsible for all the phases. This allows for a lot more flexibility. Lean Six Sigma also had a scalability advantage. This allowed time for such things as understanding employee buy-in and developing leadership skills. The other appealing thing about combining Lean with Six Sigma was the attention to teams. It utilized the Jim Collins platform of getting the right people on the right bus on the right seats.

My journey to get managers and leaders on board with the concept of Lean Six Sigma took an interesting turn. I noticed the departments I managed began to fall into two separate camps. Camp One still found Lean Six Sigma a little too difficult and did an enormous amount of complaining.

Camp Two went to the other side of the continuum. They took classes, they read literature. They started having philosophical conversations with me about some of the great people that had started the process improvement movement, which included individuals such as Edwards Deming and Joseph Juran. They corrected people on the misuse of tools and, unfortunately, this cycled back to more meetings on team difficulties, failed expectations of employees, leadership problems and the lack of employee motivation. Only now, it had to do with "all those people who were not getting with the program and/or were not using the tools correctly."

The employees who had become fascinated with Lean Six Sigma started memorizing massive blocks of information. They felt they needed to mentor the other employees into submission. I realized we somehow missed the people boat. Some managers spent hours making their process maps beautiful, 3-D and colorful. Other converts insisted on building elaborate templates and putting bureaucracy in place that would force people to do the Lean thing.

I had a deep-rooted belief that there had to be a happy medium. This was the beginning of my journey to make Lean, *Leaner*. The trek continues in this work, *Leaner* Six Sigma: Making Lean Six Sigma Easier and Adaptable to Current Workplaces.

Thank you for having an open mind and a willingness to simplify this life-changing methodology. I wish you well on your *Leaner* journey!

Terra Vanzant Stern, PhD

Author

Terra Vanzant Stern, PhD, PMP, SPHR/ GPHR, has published several books and white papers on process improvement, critical thinking and leadership. Dr. Stern is a Six Sigma Master Black Belt and principal of SSD Global Solutions—**S**mart, **S**imple **D**ecision-Making. She is a popular instructor on IT-Pro TV, as well as Udemy. Dr. Stern supports a mixture of adult learning platforms to simplify all topics related to problem solving and critical thinking.

The main mission of SSD Global Solutions and Dr. Stern's efforts are to make Lean Six Sigma easier. All the programs at SSD Global Solutions concentrate on problem-solving skills and critical thinking. SSD's training program is known as *Leaner* Six Sigma (LrSS©) and is an approach to make Lean Six Sigma immediately applicable to the workplace. It is also used to simplify the certification process.

To learn more about the training programs go to: www.SSDGlobal.net

ABOUT SSD GLOBAL SOLUTIONS

SSD GLOBAL SOLUTIONS, INC, Smart, Simple Decision-Making (SSD) began in 1996, as an international global and mergers acquisitions firm. In 2004, many companies who were previously invested in growing their businesses, decided to tighten their belts due to the economic climate. This was a great opportunity for SSD to introduce Lean Six Sigma to their existing customers!

SSD remained committed to making Lean Six Sigma easier for students to understand and achieve success. The company's principal, Terra Vanzant Stern, PhD, served as the ASQ Lean Enterprise Division Chair and met many people interested in simplifying Lean Six Sigma concepts. Dr. Stern embarked on a mission to make Lean, *Leaner*. As a result, Dr. Stern has written several books and white papers on topics related to critical thinking, problem solving, project management and leadership available on Amazon.com and at major bookstores.

SSD's primary products are now all based on *Leaner* Six Sigma (LrSS©). This includes workshops on Lean and Agile Project Management and other courses related to problem solving and critical thinking.

To learn more about Dr. Stern and her Lean journey, as well as, SSD's award-winning training programs please visit: www.SSDGlobal.net.

Section I

The Basics—Making Things Better, Faster or More Cost Effective

1

What Is Process Improvement?

Without continual growth and progress, such words as improvement, achievement and success have no meaning.

Benjamin Franklin

We call our approach in this book, *Leaner* Six Sigma (*Leaner*) and often refer to it as the acronym LrSS©. However, the basic Body of Knowledge, related to Lean Six Sigma, doesn't change. *Leaner* is simply the approach to make the information more digestible and easier to understand. To simplify this text, we often use the term *Leaner* Practitioner and/or Project Manager as an umbrella term for all the various Lean Six Sigma belt designations.

The fastest way to understand how to simplify Lean Six Sigma and the value of the *Leaner* approach is to consider the definition and purpose of process improvement along with the various forms that it takes. The intent of process improvement is to identify an existing process that can be made better, faster and more cost effective. Lesson one is that *Leaner* would add the qualifier "within reason." Technically, in our evolving world, everything could be made better. So, the *Leaner* approach would promote identifying an existing process or activity that, within reason, could be made better, faster or more cost effective.

Leaner also emphasizes that once something is made better or faster it still needs to be cost effective. But the tools to make something better or faster are different than tools associated with money. So, the *Leaner* Practitioner needs to meet the need to be better or faster first and then determine the cost effectiveness. Part of the *Leaner* program is explaining how to interpret better or faster into a financial statement of reflecting Return-on-Investment.

The history of process improvement is important. However, it is often more interesting after Lean Six Sigma is implemented. But a little background information is necessary. The following chapters will provide summaries of the core concepts behind popular process improvement programs.

Initially, Lean Six Sigma was promoted as a blend of two popular methodologies, Lean and Six Sigma. The reality was that the original Lean Six Sigma programs were primarily Six Sigma with an influence of Lean. It was never a 50-50 relationship. However, over the years, Lean has certainly gained momentum. The new Lean Six Sigma is a blend of many methodologies to include not only Lean and Six Sigma, but also Agile as well as basic Project Management.

Lean Six Sigma is often referred to as a process improvement program. It is much more than that and certainly the newer versions of Lean Six Sigma have evolved into management systems and leadership development. Once again, the *Leaner* approach makes the vast amount of information easier to understand. This chapter first explains the basics of process improvement and then the following chapters summarize the basics of Lean, Agile and basic Project Management. Because Six Sigma still plays the largest role in Lean Six Sigma, it is the primary methodology, Six Sigma will be discussed in depth throughout the rest of this book.

Process improvement (PI) is a theory about how we can make existing activities better, faster or more cost effective. In other words, how can we improve things we already do and hopefully keep improving them? There are several PI theories. They all come with their own methodologies and tools and in many cases specific templates for purchase.

There are organizations and associations that specialize in sponsoring a specific PI program. These groups have long histories, politics and Bodies of Knowledge supporting that their way is the best way and these entities remain on-going.

Eventually, however, most business professionals and leaders agreed that there was not a one-size-fits-all plan. Not surprisingly, it turns out that having a plan is, almost always, better than not having a plan. Therefore, implementing any PI program can have amazing results. Six Sigma and Lean remain the top choices. But, combining the major concepts of both methodologies is more powerful.

Today, a person may become certified in Six Sigma or Lean through a variety of vendors or universities. However, the trend is overwhelming to participate in training programs that combine both Lean and Six Sigma methodologies, this combined science is known as Lean Six Sigma (LSS).

Lean Six Sigma, sometimes called Lean and Six Sigma, has done a tremendous job in increasing Return-on-Investment. But, almost 2 decades later, it is time for the next generation. We've learned ways to make the core methodology and tools better, faster and more cost effective. So, we are past due for an upgrade.

SSD Global Solutions product, *Leaner* Six Sigma (LrSS©) is that next generation. LrSS© or, if preferred, *Leaner*, simplifies the thoughts, concepts and the terms used in ordinary Lean Six Sigma programs. Using *Leaner*, students can apply models and theories, on the fly, without constantly consulting huge or complicated manuals. This is because the information is simplified in a way that it makes sense the first time it is heard. Then, immediately, the notion is tied to an activity that is meaningful and easy to recall.

This abridged and accelerated approach allows the reader or student more time to work with the context of the issue as opposed to memorizing convoluted and sometimes outdated tools. With the new push, in our society, that less education may represent more time to reason things out by discussing issues, *Leaner* is a timely addition to the problem-solving and innovation arena.

Both Six Sigma and Lean Six Sigma are problem-solving models that allow for maximum Return-on-Investment by making existing activities better, faster or more cost effective by using methodologies and tools designed for those specific purposes.

It is important to note that many organizations informally embrace the basic concepts. Many Lean and Six Sigma tools are now integrated into day-to-day business activities. Used together, Lean and Six Sigma increases the likelihood of success. Since Lean works to eliminate or reduce waste and Six Sigma works to eliminate or reduce mistakes, the methodologies are not mutually exclusive and work well together. This combined use in the industry is referred to as Lean Six Sigma (LSS).

The premise of this book is that LSS, although incredibly successful in its time, is ready for an upgrade. SSD Global Solutions *Leaner* Six Sigma (LrSS©) is *that* next generation. Like any software or game release, *Leaner* allows the foundational knowledge to be used and applied more easily with less rules and instructions.

The words of Tom Peters are so simplistic and beautiful when it comes to the concept of process improvement: "Almost all quality improvement comes via a simplification of design, manufacturing, layout, processes and procedures."

2

A Brief History of Lean and Six Sigma

The *Leaner* Practitioner who would like to apply *Leaner* and more agile concepts should understand the history of both Lean and Agile, as well as all the various forms of traditional Project Management.

This chapter is designed to give a brief history of Lean and Six Sigma. Six Sigma is covered more specifically in Chapter 5. It is the primary methodology for the *Leaner* Practitioner. This chapter provides a generally accepted historical summary. However, many individuals played a role in the formation of both Lean and Six Sigma.

Six Sigma was developed by Motorola in 1981, to reduce defects. During the 1980s, it spread to recognized companies including General Electric and AlliedSignal. Six Sigma incorporated Total Quality Management (TQM) as well as Statistical Process Control (SPC) and expanded from a manufacturing focus to other industries and processes. Motorola documented more than $16 billion in savings. This is when many other companies decided to adopt the methodology. Naturally, the Six Sigma methodology has evolved over time. A core belief is that manufacturing and business processes share characteristics that can be measured, analyzed, improved and controlled.

In 1988, Motorola won the Malcolm Baldrige National Quality Award (MBNQA) for its Six Sigma program. Six Sigma promotes the following concepts:

- Critical-to-Quality: Attributes of the most importance to the customer
- Defect: Failing to deliver what the customer wants
- Process Capability: What the process can deliver
- Variation: What the customer sees and feels
- Stable Operations: Ensuring consistent, predictable processes to improve what the customer sees and feels
- Design for Six Sigma: Designing to meet customer needs and process capability

General Electric (GE) reported $2 billion in savings attributable to Six Sigma in their 2001 annual report. Some accounts claim that GE was the catalyst will for making the methodology popular as well as enhancing the model.

They discussed the completion of over 6,000 Six Sigma projects and their probability of yielding over $3 billion in savings, by conservative estimates. Other early adopters of Six Sigma include:

- Bank of America
- Bechtel
- Borusan
- Brunswick Corporation
- DuPont
- EDS
- Honeywell
- Idex
- Raytheon
- Shaw Industries
- Smith and Nephew
- Starwood (Westin, Sheraton, Meridian)
- Wildcard Systems

The term, Sigma, is a statistical measurement based on Defects per Million Opportunities (DPMO). A defect is defined as any non-conformance of quality. At Six Sigma only 3.4 DPMO may occur. In order to use sigma as a measurement, there must be something to count and everyone must agree on what constitutes a defect. Normal distribution models look at 3 Sigma, which is essentially 6,210 DPMO. Some processes are acceptable at lower sigma levels and, in many cases, 6 Sigma is considered an ideal. Sigma (σ) is a symbol from the Greek alphabet that is used in statistics when measuring variability. In the Six Sigma methodology, a company's performance is measured by the sigma level. Sigma levels are a measurement of error rates. It costs money to fix errors, so saving this expense can be directly transferred to the bottom line.

Standard tools used in a Six Sigma workshop include:

- Process Mapping
- Affinity Diagram or Kawakita Jiro (KJ) method
- Measurement System Analysis or MSA

- Pareto Chart
- SIPOC Analysis—Supplier-Input-Process-Output-Customer
- Scatter Diagram or Scatter Plot
- Quality Function Deployment or QFD, also known as House of Quality
- Ishikawa Diagram or Fishbone
- Failure Mode Effects Analysis or FMEA
- Failure Mode and Effects Criticality Analysis or FMECA
- Value Chain Map
- Histogram
- Control Plan

Lean Manufacturing is a production practice that concentrates on the elimination of waste. It is based on the Total Production System (TPS), introduced originally by Toyota and is based on the principals of TQM. TQM capitalizes on the involvement of management, workforce, suppliers and even customers, in order to meet or exceed customer expectations.

Originally, Lean identified the following as the worst forms of waste:

- Transportation
- Inventory (all components, work-in-progress and finished product not being processed)
- Movement
- Waiting
- Over Production
- Over Processing
- Defects
- Skills

An easy way to remember the primary of waste is T-I-M W-O-O-D-S.

Eventually, Lean evolved to consider additional forms of waste. Lean Thinking is designed to:

- Shrink lead times
- Save turnover expenses
- Reduce setup times
- Avoid unnecessary expenses
- Increase profits

Lean focuses on getting the right things, to the right place, at the right time, in the right quantity while minimizing waste. Lean also makes the work simple enough to understand, to do and to manage. The very nature of Lean would suggest that it would be "wasteful," to spend time trying to understand complicated manuals or processes, so it is best to simplify language.

Typical tools promoted in Lean include:

- 5S
- Error Proofing
- Current Reality Trees
- Conflict Resolution Diagram
- Future Reality Diagram
- Inventory Turnover Rate
- Just in Time (JIT)—drop theories
- Kaizen
- Kanban
- Lean Metric
- One-Piece Flow
- Overall Effectiveness
- Prerequisite Tree
- Process Route Table
- Quick Changeover
- Standard Rate or Work
- Takt Time
- Theory of Constraints
- Total Productive Maintenance
- Toyota Production System
- Transition Tree
- Value-Added to Non-Value-Added Lead Time Ratio
- Value Stream Mapping
- Value Stream Costing
- Visual Management
- Workflow Diagram

Another variation of Lean is Lean Office. There are seven primary principles to a Lean Office. These are continually being updated:

1. Committed Leadership
2. Establishing Metrics and Goals

3. Standardized Processes
4. 5S—a physical organizational system
5. Minimal Work in Progress (WIP)
6. Positive Workflow
7. An Understanding of Demand

In the early 1990s, Six Sigma and Lean independently recognized that their core methodologies and tools could be used for "services" as well as manufacturing. Then, in the late 1990s, AlliedSignal and Maytag autonomously began experimenting with using Six Sigma concepts in tandem with Lean theories. Many leaders and managers formally acknowledged that Six Sigma and Lean were not competing methodologies. One of the most powerful advantages of using both Six Sigma and Lean included the fact that both methods used the same set of analytical tools. For example, Six Sigma used Pareto Charts, a popular analytical tool, to identify mistakes/defects. Lean utilized the Pareto Chart to identify waste. However, the dynamics of creating a Pareto Chart were the same.

Other industries rapidly realized the value of using both methodologies. The term Lean and Six Sigma became common. Eventually this term morphed into Lean Six Sigma. Lean Six Sigma may be used but not limited to:

- Construction
- Education
- Finance
- Government
- Healthcare
- Hospitality
- Insurance

Lean Six Sigma is about increasing quality and profit. The new tools include methodologies based on teamwork as a principle. Process improvement is not a linear process where each component is handed-off to another department or individual. Each member of the process is involved in improving client satisfaction.

As noted earlier, *Leaner* Six Sigma supports all of the same principals and appreciates all of the contributions and history supporting both Six Sigma and Lean. *Leaner* just makes understanding less complex. The new *Leaner* tools focus on Continuous Improvement as a guiding principle.

The road to quality is paved with small incremental improvements. Major sweeping changes seldom work. As this country moves its business style from control to management to leadership, we are finding that the people doing the work are the most capable of identifying changes necessary to improve quality. Leadership must listen and implement changes rather than direct the solutions. Some examples are:

- Improving Forecast Accuracy
- Reducing Volume of Rejected Orders
- Improving Consumer Loan Cycle Time
- Reducing Engine Installation Times
- Eliminating Mistakes in an Operating Room
- Reducing Pharmacy Dispensing Error Rates
- Improving the Effectiveness of Employee Hazard Recognition
- Reducing Process Variation Costs Related to Manufacturing

Before examining Lean Six Sigma, the topic of Continuous Improvement (CI) programs should be explored. Most companies have some sort of quality control program. These programs may be formal or informal. Most programs have specific documents and manuals. However, other quality programs are informal and not tracked or recorded. Quality is obviously a large piece of continual improvement. All CI programs ask two questions: (1) Who are the Customers? and (2) What will it take to satisfy them?

Lean and Six Sigma both endorse the Plan-Do-Check-Act (PDCA) Model. This popular project management tool is easy to understand. It is also called the Deming Wheel or Deming Cycle.

- Plan: Identify an Opportunity and Plan for Change
- Do: Implement the Change on a Small Scale
- Check: Use Data to Analyze the Results of the Change and Determine Whether It Made a Difference
- Act: If the Change Was Successful, Implement It on a Wider Scale and Continuously Assess the Results. If the Change Did Not Work, Begin the Cycle Again

Both Lean and Six Sigma support the idea of Continuous Improvement (CI). It is an ongoing effort to improve products, services or processes. It can be incremental improvement (over time) or breakthrough improvement (all at once). CI programs often are not proactive and are presented with a problem up front. Within any problem-solving model, there are four steps to remember: Define the Problem, Generate the Solution, Evaluate and Select an Alternative and Implement.

Lean Six Sigma uses a set of quality tools that are often used in TQM. These tools sometimes referred to as problem-solving tools include:

- Control Charts
- Pareto Diagrams
- Process Mapping
- Root Cause Analysis
- SPC

Lean Six Sigma largely depends on the Define-Measure-Analyze-Improve-Control (DMAIC) model. This model, initially developed by Motorola, later was enhanced by General Electric (GE). Some historical documents claim that GE was responsible for the creation or at least the modification of the *Define* phase. Companies often modify the phases to include industry specific goals. Summarized, most companies agree, on these basics:

- Define the process improvement goals that are consistent with customer demands and enterprise strategy
- Measure (audit) the current process and collect relevant data for future comparison
- Analyze and examine the information received in the audit performed in Measure
- Improve or optimize the process based upon the analysis
- Control to ensure that any variances are corrected before they result in defects

Lean Six Sigma uses the tools above. It also uses the martial arts designations: White, Yellow, Green, Black and Master Black Belt, to denote the level of expertise. The generally accepted belt designations are as follows:

- White Belts—individuals who have been given a basic orientation
- Yellow Belts—individuals trained in the basic application of Lean Six Sigma management tools
- Green Belts—individuals who handle Lean Six Sigma implementation along with their other regular job responsibilities

- Black Belts—individuals who devote up to 100% of their time to Lean Six Sigma initiatives
- Master Black Belts—individuals who act in a teaching, mentoring and coaching role

Leaner suggests a much easier understanding of this summarized model:

- Define—Understand the process that needs to be made better, faster and more cost effective.
- Measure—Get a snapshot of what is happening now. What is the current state, now, eliminating all bias.
- Analyze—Ask why the current state is the way it is—recognize that with this new information from Measure, there may be an automatic process improvement. Now, many things have been exposed.
- Improve—Build a project plan around the improvement with one of the solutions discovered from Analyze.
- Control—Determine how to keep this process improvement in place.

The roles, responsibility and education for Lean Six Sigma Green Belts and Black Belts are the most consistent. The major difference between a Green Belt and a Black Belt is that Green Belt has a regular job where they apply process improvement via Lean Six Sigma, whereas a Black Belt may be engaged solely in the process improvement effort. To be a successful Green Belt, individual expertise must be blended with Lean Six Sigma tools and methods.

To be a successful Black Belt or Master Black Belt requires an overall understanding of business usually in combination with a Master of Business Administration degree. An Information Technologist, who by nature must interface with various departments or individuals who have owned their own business, are often excellent candidates for Lean Six Sigma Black Belt studies. Black Belts and Green Belts both need to have a valid understanding of basic project management.

Other roles in the Lean Six Sigma organization include Sponsor, Process Owner and Cross-Functional Teams. The sponsor is generally the person paying for the project. The process owner is the person normally responsible for the process success and the cross-functional team is the ideal team promoted by Lean Six Sigma—a team made up of multiple disciplines to include functional expertise, finance, marketing and operations.

The roles and responsibilities in Lean Six Sigma are still rooted in TQM. In a TQM effort, all members of an organization participate in improving processes, products and services. TQM practices are based on cross-functional product design and process management. Other components related to Lean Six Sigma also covered in TQM include:

- Supplier relations
- Overall quality management
- Customer and employee involvement
- Information analysis
- Feedback
- Committed leadership
- Strategic planning

The *Leaner* Practitioner interested in gaining a better understanding of the history of process improvement will benefit from studying material first presented within the TQM framework. Works by Edwards Deming and Joseph Juran are still prevalent today. Other major authors include Kaoru Ishikawa, A.V. Feigenbaum and Phillip B. Crosby.

And now for a brief history of *Leaner* Six Sigma, our aim is to simplify everything. This includes the model, the tools, the process and the presentation of results. We believe that much of the work in Lean Six Sigma has already been accomplished. Therefore, it might be okay, especially in certain circumstances, to use an MS-Excel calculator, a template, automated tools or someone else's expertise when completing a project. *Leaner* believes in the collective intelligence of teams and sharing information and learning from each other. In other words, sometimes it is necessary to make a cake from scratch, but sometimes using a cake mix or simply purchasing the pastry makes more sense. How the results are achieved is not nearly as important as achieving the results.

To a certain extent, *Leaner* believes that it is not always necessary to work hard to get meaningful results—sometimes it's just about working smarter, paying attention to what is already available in tapping into *Leaner* Practitioner critical thinking skills.

Applying basic process improvement in the workplace appears primarily in the following examples:

- Mapping the processes
- Analyzing the processes
- Redesigning the processes

- Acquiring the right resources
- Implementing and communicating the change
- Reviewing the processes for results

The *Leaner* Practitioner is a person who capitalizes on all the information available and makes a choice about which tools are the most appropriate to make an existing process better, faster or more cost effective.

3

Agile

Learn from yesterday, live for today, hope for tomorrow. The important thing is not to stop questioning.

Albert Einstein

The advantage of learning Agile Project Management in a book dedicated to *Leaner* practices is multifaceted. First, the *Leaner* Practitioner may find themselves in an agile environment. Secondly, there are so many synergies between the approach to Lean Six Sigma regarding people management related to Agile that will make learning *Leaner*. And, finally, Agile practices in project management are becoming more and more popular. A *Leaner* Practitioner who can demonstrate that they understand the agile environment and are in fact willing to be agile themselves is an enormous benefit to their resume.

The genesis of Agile is found in a group of software development methodologies. These methodologies are based on iterative development, where requirements and solutions evolve through collaborative effort. Agile software development models support self-organizing, cross-functional teams. It isn't surprising that this morphed into a structure for project management.

The approach to Agile Project Management is very foreign to traditional project management administration. It is possible, however, for all project managers to benefit from Agile techniques. This is especially true for the *Leaner* Practitioner. Many of the tools and methods can easily be incorporated into certain projects. This would include military project management, even though at first glance this would not seem possible.

It is important to know a little about the history and evolution of Agile. Throughout this book, Agile techniques will be discussed more fully, but this chapter is dedicated to understanding Agile as a stand-alone methodology.

Agile theory is based on an Agile Manifesto. Sometimes, a manifesto is confused with the term "Body of Knowledge" (BOK). Whereas there are some synergies between what we consider a body of knowledge, as presented in other disciplines such as project management, a manifesto is more about purpose than technicalities.

The Agile Manifesto was written in February of 2001 at a summit of 17 independent-minded practitioners. Most of the participants had a programming background. According to the Agile Alliance, many participants had a different idea of what constituted Agile theory. However, they did agree on four main values:

- **Individuals and interactions** over processes and tools
- **Working software** over comprehensive documentation
- **Customer collaboration** over contract negotiation
- **Responding to change** over following a plan

These four values were intended to supplement the Agile Twelve Principles. History on how these 12 principles were developed originally remains a bit fuzzy. Still, these items provide a better understanding of the framework and intention of Agile methods. The principles are defined as followed:

1. Our highest priority is to satisfy the customer through early and continuous delivery of valuable software
2. Welcome changing requirements, even late in development. Agile processes harness change for the customer's competitive advantage
3. Deliver working software frequently; from a couple of weeks to a couple of months, with a preference to the shorter timescale
4. Business people and developers must work together daily throughout the project
5. Build projects around motivated individuals. Give them the environment and support they need and trust them to get the job done
6. The most efficient and effective method of conveying information to and within a development team is face-to-face conversation
7. Working software is the primary measure of progress
8. Agile processes promote sustainable development. The sponsors, developers and users should be able to maintain a constant pace indefinitely

9. Continuous attention to technical excellence and good design enhances agility

10. Simplicity—the art of maximizing the amount of work not done—is essential

11. The best architectures, requirements and designs emerge from self-organizing teams

12. At regular intervals, the team reflects on how to become more effective, then tunes and adjusts its behavior accordingly

Lean, as addressed in the previous chapter, does not technically have a manifesto or a specific industry agreed-upon list of principles. However, much of Lean Thinking is based on Edwards Deming's 14 Points from his book *Out of the Crisis*. These points provide for a good comparison between Lean Thinking and Agile Techniques as Agile supports many of Dr. Deming's unprecedented points. Dr. Deming taught that most quality issues were systemic (process related) and, therefore, the responsibility of management. Here are the summarized points:

1. Create devotion of purpose toward the improvement of product and service. With the aim to become competitive, stay in business and to provide jobs

2. Adopt the new philosophies. Management must awaken to the challenge, must learn their responsibilities and take on leadership for change

3. Cease dependence on inspection to achieve quality. Eliminate the need for massive inspection by building quality into the product in the first place

4. End the practice of awarding business based on a price tag. Instead, minimize total cost

5. Move toward a single supplier for any one item—loyalty and trust are important

6. Improve constantly, forever, the system of production and service to improve quality and productivity and thus constantly decrease costs

7. Institute training on the job

8. Drive out fear

9. Eliminate slogans, exhortations and targets for the work force asking for zero defects and new levels of productivity. Such exhortations only create adversarial relationships, as the bulk of the causes of low quality and low productivity belong to the system and thus lie beyond the power of the work force

10. Eliminate work standards (quotas) on the factory floor. Substitute leadership
11. Eliminate management by objective. Eliminate management by numbers, numerical goals. Substitute leadership
12. Remove barriers that discount the hourly worker of his right to pride of workmanship. The responsibility of supervisors must be changed from sheer numbers to quality
13. Remove barriers that discount people of their right to pride of workmanship
14. Institute a vigorous program of education and self-improvement
15. Put everyone in the company to work to accomplish the transformation. The transformation is everyone's job

RECOGNIZED CERTIFICATIONS IN AGILE

How individuals define the Body of Knowledge (BOK) for Agile can be confusing. Generally, any type of legitimate certification is based on a BOK. However, Agile has many methodologies such as Scrum, XP, Lean, FDD, Crustal, DSDM and even references to Just-in-Time Kanban philosophies.

Proving a comprehensive BOK, covering all the ideas and concepts that drive Agile is not possible, yet. This means that several special certifications exist through private vendors. However, the most respected and standardized one is that provided by the Project Management Institute (PMI).

The Project Management Institute offers a PMI Agile Certified Practitioner (PMI-ACP)® designed to formally recognize an individual's knowledge of agile principles and skills with agile techniques.

The prerequisites to sit for this exam include, but may not be limited to:

- 2,000 hours of general project experience working on teams. A current PMP® or PgMP® will satisfy this requirement, but is not required to apply for the PMI-ACP.
- 1,500 hours working on agile project teams or with agile methodologies. This requirement is in addition to the 2,000 hours of general project experience.
- 21 contact hours of training in agile practices.

Other recognized entities that provide well-respected certifications in Agile include, but are not limited to:

Agile Alliance: The Agile Alliance is the original global agile community, with a mission to help advance agile principles and practices, regardless of methodology.

Scrum Alliance: The Scrum Alliance is a non-profit professional membership organization that promotes understanding and usage of Scrum. The Scrum Alliance offers several professional certifications:
- Certified Scrum Master (CSM)
- Certified Scrum Product Owner (CSPO)
- Certified Scrum Developer (CSD)
- Certified Scrum Professional (CSP)
- Certified Scrum Coach (CSC)
- Certified Scrum Trainer (CST)

Platinum Edge: The Platinum Edge are the providers of training classes worldwide and developers of transition strategies and coaching for organizations moving to more agile project management platforms.

AGILE BASIC TOOLS AND TECHNIQUES

Probably the most recognized word when Agile is applied to project management is Scrum. Scrum is an Agile methodology that can be applied to nearly any project. Although originally used for software development, Scrum theory is now used in all types of business ventures.

Scrum Model

The Scrum model advises that each sprint begins with a brief planning meeting and closes with a review. Scrum is a management and control process that cuts through complexity and is a simple framework for effective team collaboration.

Starting with a basic daily Scrum, there are three questions the project manager, sometimes referred to as the Scrum Master, will ask the Scrum team:

1. What was necessary to do yesterday?
2. What is necessary do today?
3. Are there any impediments in the way?

The Scrum team, ideally, includes everyone who touches the project. These meetings are held in an area where everyone can stand and face each other, generally in a circle. The purpose of team players standing is to promote that the session should be quick and precise. Scrum sessions are held for individual projects. However, the Scrum meeting could support a daily report out, as well as reports on various projects.

By focusing on what each person accomplished yesterday and will accomplish today, the team gains an excellent understanding of what work has been done and what work remains to be done. Sometimes to make this easier, the Scrum master may refer to a Burndown Chart. However, this chart may also be used to show the progress of a Sprint discussed in the next section. See Figures 3.1 and 3.2 for Burndown Chart examples.

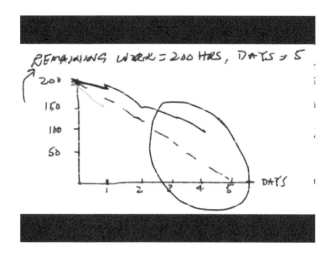

FIGURE 3.1
Example of Burndown chart—Manual.

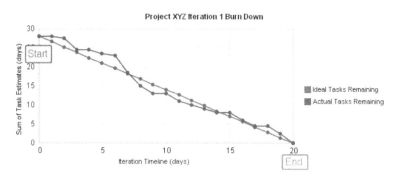

FIGURE 3.2
Example of Burndown chart—Computer generated.

The Scrum Master does everything possible to help the team perform at their highest level. This involves removing any impediments to progress, facilitating meetings and doing things like working with the product owner to make sure the product backlog is in good shape.

Sprints

In the Scrum version of Agile, Sprints are collections of work confined to a regular, repeatable work cycle, known as a sprint or iteration. These iterations can be anywhere from one-week to 30 days, but should be the same duration. This allows for less to remember about the sprint schedule and the planning becomes more accurate. During this time, the Scrum team works on very specific and agreed upon work. Nothing can be changed during the Sprint.

Step One is a Sprint Planning session. Everyone who touches the process should be involved. Whereas daily Scrum meetings typically include those doing the work who will report out to other interested parties if appropriate, for a Sprint to be successful, everyone should be involved. Naturally, this would be when a consensus should be reached about the Sprint duration. The optimum Sprint duration depends on many factors to include, but not be limited to, availability of resources and urgency of the project.

Step Two is to decide what piece of the backlog should be tackled first. Most Sprints include a little more than can be achieved which is why some employees are not as comfortable as others with the process.

Once the body of work is agreed upon, tasks are taken one-by-one, in logical order and the objectives of the first Sprint are determined.

Sprint Retrospectives

Sprint Retrospectives are meetings at the end of each sprint where the Scrum team discusses what went well, what could change and how to make any changes. Typical questions for discussion include:

- What went well during the sprint cycle?
- What went wrong during the sprint cycle?
- What could we do differently to improve?

Agile Stages

It may be easier to think of the Agile process in terms of steps or stages once the terminology is understood.

Stage One: The Product or Process Owner identifies the vision.

Stage Two: The Scrum Master or Product/Process Owner creates the roadmap. The roadmap is the high-level view.

Stage Three: The Scrum Master or the Product/Process Owner releases a plan identifying the timetable.

Stage Four: Product/Process Owner, the Scrum Master and the Scrum Team plan the Sprints. Sprint planning takes place at the beginning of each Sprint.

Stage Five: During each Sprint, there are daily Scrum Meetings that last no longer than 15 minutes.

Stage Six: At the end of every Sprint, a report is given to the product/process Stakeholders.

Stage Seven: The Team holds a Sprint Retrospective.

AGILE MANUFACTURING

The term Agile Manufacturing was watermarked by Francois de Villiers in his work, *Lean and Agile World Class Manufacturing*. Villiers mentions that his work was never meant to be published. He said that he had compiled the manual as a personal self-help text. It did, however, evolve into this sophisticated account of both Lean and Agile Manufacturing.

Villiers describes Agile Manufacturing as tools, techniques and initiatives that enable a plant or company to thrive under conditions of unpredictable change. Agile manufacturing not only enables a plant to achieve rapid response to customer needs, but also includes the ability to quickly reconfigure operations—and strategic alliances—to respond rapidly to unforeseen shifts in the marketplace. In some instances, it also incorporates "mass customization" concepts to satisfy unique customer requirements. In broad terms, it includes the ability to react quickly to technical or environmental surprises. It is a means of thriving in an environment of continuous change, by managing complex inter and intra-firm relationships through innovations in technology, information, communication, organizational redesign and new marketing strategies.

AGILE PROJECT MANAGEMENT

Agile Project Management promotes a value-driven approach that allows project managers to deliver high-priority, high-quality work. It is an iterative, incremental method of managing the design and building activities. It works well in engineering and information technology.

Agile methods are mentioned in the *Guide to the Project Management Body of Knowledge* (*PMBOK Guide*) under the Project Lifecycle definition and are referred to as an adaptive project life cycle. Typically, adaptive life cycles are iterative and incremental. The caveat is that the iterations in Agile processes are rapid—2 weeks to 3 weeks in length—with fixed resources.

Applying Agile techniques in the workforce takes various forms:

- Understanding the value of cross functional teams
- Scrum meetings designed to meet with the staff responsible for the project daily
- Looking at project development as an incremental approach
- Creating collaborative timeframes for project items to be completed

This quote is anonymous, however, a great way to end this chapter: "Agile is about doing as opposed to being paralyzed by over planning." A core principle of agile is working in a constant pace which in turn enables *the Leaner* Practitioner to deliver at a constant pace.

4

Project Management

Let our advance worrying become advanced thinking and planning.

Winston Churchill

In my book, *Lean and Agile Project Management* (Taylor & Francis 2017), it is noted that many people are not aware of the various forms of project management. And that, most project managers (PMs) are surprised to learn that there are three primary recognized bodies of knowledge for project management: PMBOK®, PRINCE2® and the International Organization for Standardization (ISO) 21500.

Because this work is trying to portray a *Leaner* education concerning Project Management, this chapter simply capitalizes on the parallels of the three primary bodies of knowledge and speaks to their similarities rather than their differences. There are, however, many other recognized bodies of knowledge in the world of Project Management. The following material discusses only the primary bodies of knowledge. A basic understanding helps the *Leaner* Practitioner integrate Project Management into all facets of the process improvement. The *Leaner* Practitioner understands that all viable process improvements eventually become a project to complete. At that point, the *Leaner* Practitioner becomes a project manager.

If the *Leaner* Practitioner knows how to make the process better, faster and more cost effective immediately, there is no need to engage in the critical thinking and problem-solving exercises promoted by Lean Six Sigma. The Practitioner can go directly to creating a project. This is the leanest thing to do. Often, however, the solution is not apparent. Therefore, process improvement tools that focus on reasoning exercises are so important.

Regardless if the *Leaner* Practitioner knows how to solve the problem immediately or needs to engage in critical thinking tools to figure it out, at some point, the process improvement becomes a project. Understanding the various forms of project management theory is useful.

This chapter begins with a summary explanation of the primary Project Management Bodies of Knowledges typically used in business today.

> ***The Project Management Body of Knowledge (PMBOK®)***, is a U.S.-based program supported by the Project Management Institute (PMI). It provides a set of standard terminology and guidelines. Although it overlaps with practices used in general management, there are several unique thoughts such as critical path and work breakdown structure not typically discussed in other management disciples such as financial forecasting or organizational development. PMI offers individual certification programs.

> ***Projects in Controlled Environments, version 2 (PRINCE2®)***, is a program that began as a joint venture between the UK government and a private company, Capita. PRINCE2® focuses on dividing projects into manageable and controllable phases. It encompasses Quality Management and offers individual certification programs.

> ***ISO 21500:2012, Guidance on Project Management***, is an international standard developed by the International Organization for Standardization (ISO). An interesting piece of trivia is that work began on this standard in 2007, but it was not officially published until 2012, making it the newest of the three primary bodies. This standard is the first of the intended series of standards and align by design with other more established standards in areas such as Quality Management Systems (QMS) and Risk Management. Currently, it is considered a guideline so there is no official certification or registration process.

One commonality in all three primary bodies is the concept of a Project Life Cycle (PLC). The PLC refers to a series of activities which are necessary to fulfill project goals or objectives. It is more commonly known as the Project Management Life Cycle (PMLC).

The Project Management Life Cycle has six phases: Initiation, Planning, Execution, Monitoring, Controlling and Closure. Some bodies of knowledge (BOK) do not specifically name these steps specifically and/or combine them with other phases. Named or not, a successful project must go through each phase of the cycle.

To summarize the steps/phases in the cycle, the term Initiation refers to selecting the goal. Planning the project involves estimating resources and time, identifying the order of tasks, determining the execution schedule and performing a risk assessment. Execution, simply stated, involves performing the tasks. Monitoring and Controlling occur during all phases of the project. It includes monitoring resources, quality, risks and overall project status. Closing is the phase that includes all the activities necessary for the project office to bring closure to the project effort.

Project Management begins with closely observing each phase of the PMLC and envisioning *Leaner* opportunities. This is a summary of the phases and how certain tools might be used. A more in-depth discussion on each of the phases occurs later in this book.

PROJECT INITIATION

The Project Initiation Phase is the most crucial phase in the PMLC. This phase establishes the scope. A major outcome is the project charter. A charter is typically developed by creating a business case followed by conducting a feasibility study. If there is more than one resource available to execute the project, a project team is established. There may also be a need to establish or partner with the Project Management Office (PMO). There are several Lean opportunities.

A Supplier-Input-Process-Output-Customer (SIPOC) analysis could be used in either the business case or feasibility study. This would identify all the stakeholders in the project and consider the non-human resources that may contribute to the success of the project. Using a template to create the project charter is another simple way to make the process Lean. The Plan-Do-Check-Act (PDCA) methodology may be the best way to establish a PMO.

PROJECT PLANNING

Many aspects of project management come down to good planning. These diagrams discussed later in this work include, but are not limited to:

- The KJ Method or Affinity Diagrams
- Interrelationship Digraph (ID)

- Tree Diagrams
- Prioritization Diagrams
- Matrix Diagrams
- Process Decision Diagrams
- Activity Network Diagrams

There are several project management tools that may be applied in this phase. For example, suggesting a 5S model, a five-step method of organizing and maintaining workplace, prior to beginning the project, may help in the execution if the environment is physically disorganized. Gemba walks, a term used to describe personal observation of work can promote a greater understanding of constraints within the work environment.

A Key Performance Indicator (KPI) is a business metric used to evaluate factors that are crucial to the success of an organization and can vary from organization to organization. Strongly promoted KPIs can be extremely powerful drivers of behavior and may be addressed in this phase of the cycle.

Many Agile professionals suggest five levels of planning to include:

- Product or Service Vision
- Product or Service Roadmap
- Release or Rollout Plan
- Sprint Plan
- A strategy to achieve daily commitment

PROJECT EXECUTION

Initiation and Planning are necessary for efficacious execution of any project. Basic project management and Lean are in alignment with how a project should be deployed. The use of a project plan using a Work Breakdown Structure (WBS) and establishing metrics are good examples. What Lean offers not typically addressed in project management methodologies is the mistake-proofing aspect. The strategy used to ensure the success of the project often involves placing controls and detection measures within the project plan.

Visual feedback systems (Andon) may encourage quicker execution. Creating continuous flow eliminates waste and speeds the process in many projects. Andon means "Sign" or "Signal." It is a visual aid which alerts and highlights where action is required. Think, for example, a flashing light in a manufacturing plant that indicates the line has been stopped by one of the operators due to some irregularity.

In this phase, Hoshin Kanri, a policy deployment tool may help ensure that progress toward the strategic goals is consistent. Hoshin Kanri is a method for ensuring that the strategic goals of a company drive progress and action at every level within that company.

PROJECT MONITORING AND CONTROLLING

The Monitoring and Controlling process oversees all the tasks and metrics necessary to ensure that the approved and authorized project is within scope, on time and on budget so that the project proceeds with minimal risk. Both Lean and Agile methodologies promote more people interaction than typical project management. Project management models often rely more heavily on Gantt and other charts to track progress. Concentrating a little more on the people aspects will increase team accountability.

Lean specifically looks at Poka-yoke and Heijunka. Poka-yoke is the Japanese term for mistake-proofing. Mistake-proofing involves eliminating possibilities for errors. An example would be color-coding a wiring template to assist the worker. The input and output would be the same color.

Heijunka is the Japanese word for level scheduling. A level scheduling strategy's objective is to minimize disruptions caused by sudden changes in demand levels by matching the product family schedules with product-by-product schedules. To achieve the objectives of level scheduling, both the sales and production departments must agree on a fixed level of output volume and output duration.

PROJECT CLOSING

The purpose of the closing phase in the project management lifecycle is to confirm completion of project deliverables to the satisfaction of the project sponsor and to communicate final project disposition and status to all participants and stakeholders. The concept of Standardized Work is often useful during this phase. This is where documented procedures capture best practices. If Standardized Work has been created, it may be used to accelerate the closing process.

Agile project closure is much more robust and has definitive objectives such as handing the project over to operations, tidying up any loose ends, reviewing the project to a stronger extent and making celebrating an essential activity as opposed to something that is nice to do.

Lean project closure concentrates on keeping improvements on-going, documenting best practices and encouraging lessons learned meetings. It embraces brainstorming around "how can we do it better next time."

The advantage of applying *Leaner* concept to Project Management is that it incorporates stronger planning tools and various aspects of mistake-proofing not classically addressed in basic project management theory. The journey begins with examining the PMLC through a Lean perspective. Lean Project Management focuses on making projects better, faster and more cost effective by eliminating waste and unnecessary activities.

The *PMBOK®* specifically lists ten knowledge areas in project management that are addressed in a different structure within in PRINCE2® and ISO 21500:

1. Integration
2. Scope
3. Time Management
4. Cost Management
5. Quality
6. Human Resources
7. Communications
8. Risk
9. Procurement
10. Stakeholders

These ten factors, as identified in the *PMBOK®*, will be used in Part One to demonstrate how making and can be a powerful approach to enhancing accomplishments.

A chapter on the core concepts of project management would not be complete without some basic history.

In 2570 BC the Great Pyramid of Giza was completed. Although archaeologists still debate about how this amazing feat was achieved, most agree it is the first evidence of project management. There was some degree of planning, execution and control involved in managing this project.

Fast forwarding to 208 BC was the construction of the Great Wall of China. Although considered a *Wonder* of the World, there is more documentation available about this project. Labor was organized into three groups which included soldiers, common people and criminals. In the end, Emperor Qin Shi Huang ordered millions of people to finish this project.

It was not until 1917, that the idea of the use of a standard set of tools might be useful in project management. It started with the Gantt chart, developed by Henry Gantt. This tool was considered a major innovation in the 1920s. It was used with much anticipation on the Hoover Dam project which was started in 1931. Computerization and much easier to use, Gantt charts are still in use today.

After the Hoover Dam project, project management as a science developed rapidly via these key events:

- **1956**: The American Association of Cost Engineers (now AACE International)
- **1957**: The Critical Path Method (CPM) Invented by the Dupont Corporation
- **1958**: The Program Evaluation Review Technique (PERT) Invented for the U.S. Navy's Polaris Project
- **1962**: United States Department of Defense Mandate the Work Breakdown Structure (WBS) Approach
- **1965**: The International Project Management Association (IPMA) Was Founded
- **1969**: Project Management Institute (PMI) Launched to Promote the Project Management Profession

As project management matured, so did progressive thoughts and ideas. In 1984, Dr. Eliyahu Goldratt introduced a novel called *The Goal*. In this work, Dr. Goldratt addressed the Theory of Constraints (TOC). His premise was that any manageable system is limited in achieving more of its goal by a small number of constraints and there is always, at least, one constraint. The TOC process is used to identify the constraint and exam how to exploit the obstacle. The methods and algorithms from TOC went on to form the basis of Critical Chain Project Management.

In 1986, Scrum became a recognized project management style and in 1987, PMI released the first edition of the PMBOK®. Three years later, in 1989, the PRINCE method was developed.

There continues to be a bevy on new thoughts about effective project management. For example, the PMBOK® is in its 6th Edition. However, the most intriguing thing to impact basic project management, in several years, is the knowledge and ability to apply Lean concepts.

Basic project management is applied continually in the workplace. Often the management of projects is informal and there may not be a specific process in place. Ways to improve project management in the workplace even when a formal methodology is not in place include:

- Establishing firm goals and objectives
- Structured planning
- Focusing on communication
- Determining the right project management tools
- Identifying some of the small "wins"
- Document important items

5

A Deeper Dive: Six Sigma and the DMAIC Model

All improvement happens project by project and in no other way.

Joseph Juran

There are several models used in Six Sigma, but the Define-Measure-Analyze-Improve-Control (DMAIC) model is the most popular. These five phases, sometimes called steps, are the basis of most Lean Six Sigma training. This methodology allows coworkers the ability to speak the same language, track their progress and work together successfully.

Each phase (or step) of this model supports tools, ideas and templates. After each phase of the model, a tollgate review is performed. A tollgate is a check sheet to ensure activities have been completed. In *Leaner,* this has not changed. *Leaner* just made the steps easier to understand and the tools easier to use. The integrity of the program is still intact.

For example, in formal Six Sigma, it is rare to start activities on a phase until the previous phase is completed. Lean Six Sigma is a little more flexible. In other words, if there is an opportunity in *Define* to satisfy some of the *Measure* requirements, those are taken into consideration. It isn't the goal to move to one phase before the previous phase is complete, but it is allowed. Generally, this is because a Lean Six Sigma project has the same manager from cradle to grave, whereas the Six Sigma project has several owners and there may be a different resource for each phase due to the size of the project.

Leaner goes a step further. Whereas LSS offered more flexibility in the model, *Leaner* supports the idea that the model should be looked at as a guideline. Additionally, *Leaner* supports that a handful of tools is often all that is needed to successfully complete a project.

Certainly, it is nice to have additional tools, but those can be added on an as-needed basis rather than using the time that should be devoted to fixing the problem at hand memorizing outdated or unnecessary tools.

There are only a few things written in stone as far as *Leaner* is concerned. For example, a WBS is an outline where tasks are numbered 1, 2, 3. The tasks associated with each number are then labeled 1.1, 1.2 and so forth. Tasks under 1.2 would be noted as 1.2.1, 1.2.2. *Leaner* believes this to be an imperative as opposed to an option. WBS is the preferred way in both Lean and Six Sigma to create a project plan.

Here an account of the main activities in each phase of the model is discussed. In future chapters, a more in-depth, but still simplified, breakdown will be clarified.

DEFINE

Define is the first phase of the demand model. Examples of activities in this phase includes:

- Identifying, prioritizing and selecting the opportunities
- Defining the processes to be improved and preparing process maps
- Developing project team charters
- Building effective teams
- Identifying the customer segments and requirements

MEASURE

Examples of activities in the second phase of the DMAIC model include:

- Determining the parameters to be measured
- Managing the measure process
- Understanding variation

- Evaluating the measure system and selecting the measuring devices
- Determining the process performance

In the *Measure* phase consideration is given to the Critical-to-Quality factors (CTQ). CTQ is the accepted term used to define customer requirements. However, the term is also used interchangeably with Critical-to-Satisfaction and Critical-to-Success. CTQs are relevant throughout the DMAIC model.

ANALYZE

Examples of activities in the third phase of the DMAIC process include:

- Identifying potential root causes
- Implementing alternative methods
- Conducting sources of variation studies
- Conducting correlation analysis

The *Analyze* phase is crucial to the outcome. Many of the analytical problem-solving tools are utilized in this phase.

IMPROVE

Examples of fourth phase of the DMAIC model include:

- Generating solutions
- Identifying alternatives
- Ranking the alternatives
- Selecting the best solution
- Discussing the implementation aspects
- Implementing the final solution as per plan

In the *Improve* phase, implementing the best solution usually involves more than one department. Discussing the implementation aspects of the best solution with everyone impacted is a necessity before finalizing and implementation of the plan.

CONTROL

Examples of activities in the final phase include:

- Develop a control plan (specify the checkpoints and control points)
- Implement a suitable monitoring system for control
- Review and evaluate the impact of changes
- Update the documents, incorporating process changes
- Close the project, reward the team members and disband the team

In the *Control* phase, there is a check regarding data integrity. This is where a control and transition plan are written. The idea behind the control plan, which can also be a major deliverable, is that the control plan is written in a way that even those not exposed to Lean Six Sigma can review and understand it.

Success in Lean Six Sigma is not based on complicated or high-tech procedures. It relies wholly on tried and tested systems. It simplifies things by reducing the many complexities. One way to reduce complexity is to have everyone on the project team follow a basic roadmap.

There are several things a person may want to do before beginning the DMAIC process:

- Conduct a PDCA/PDSA (Plan-Do-Check-Act) or (Plan-Do-Study-Act) to make sure a DMAIC is merited
- Compile a SWOT (Strengths-Weaknesses-Opportunities-Threats) Analysis
- Perform a 5S (A physical organizational method that requires: Sorting, Setting in Order, Shining, Standardizing and Sustaining)

PDCA

PDCA (plan-do-check-act, sometimes seen as plan-do-check-adjust) is a repetitive four-stage model for continuous improvement (CI) in business process management. The **PDCA** model is also known as the Deming circle/cycle/wheel, Shewhart cycle, control circle/cycle or plan-do-study-act (PDSA).

Plan-Do-Check-Act Procedure

1. Plan: Recognize an opportunity and plan a change
2. Do: Test the change. Carry out a small-scale study
3. Check: Review the test, analyze the results and identify what was necessary to learn
4. Act: Act based on what was necessary to learn in the study step: If the change did not work, go through the cycle again with a different plan. If the *Leaner* Practitioner was successful, incorporate what you learned from the test into wider changes. Use what you learned to plan new improvements, beginning the cycle again

SWOT Analysis

A SWOT Analysis is a study undertaken by an organization to identify its internal strengths and weaknesses, as well as its external opportunities and threats.

- Strengths: Characteristics of the business or project that give it an advantage over others
- Weaknesses: Characteristics of the business that place the business or project at a disadvantage relative to others
- Opportunities: Elements in the environment that the business or project could exploit to its advantage
- Threats: Elements in the environment that could cause trouble for the business or project

5S

One of the methods of determining an organization's approach to its business is to evaluate its workplace organization capability & visual management standards.

The 5 Steps are as follows:

- **Sort**: Sort out & separate that which is needed & not needed in the area
- **Straighten** or **Set in Order**: Arrange items that are needed so that they are ready & easy to use. Clearly identify locations for all items so that anyone can find them & return them once the task is completed
- **Shine**: Clean the workplace on a regular basis in order to maintain standards & identify defects

- **Standardize**: Revisit the first three of the 5S on a frequent basis and confirm the condition of the Gemba using standard procedures
- **Sustain**: Keep to the rules to maintain the standard & continue to improve every day.

Here's a quick overview of the two methodologies that impact Lean Six Sigma.

Six Sigma

- Emphasizes the need to recognize opportunities and eliminate defects as defined by customers
- Recognizes that variation hinders our ability to reliably deliver high quality services
- Requires data driven decisions and incorporates a comprehensive set of quality tools under a powerful framework for effective problem solving
- Provides a highly prescriptive cultural infrastructure effective in obtaining sustainable results
- When implemented correctly, promises and delivers $500,000+ of improved operating profit per Black Belt per year (a hard dollar figures many companies consistently achieve)

Lean

- Focuses on maximizing process velocity
- Provides tools for analyzing process flow and delay times at each activity in a process
- Centers on the separation of "value-added" from "non-value-added" work with tools to eliminate the root causes of non-valued activities and their cost
- Focuses on reducing and/or eliminating waste

SUMMARY OVERVIEW

Lean Six Sigma is a methodology used to make things better, faster or more cost effective. It combines the best ideas captured in Six Sigma methodology and Lean thinking. Although there are many models and tools available to accomplish process improvement, there is a great deal of emphasis on the DMAIC model.

The DMAIC model phases are:

1. Define
2. Measure
3. Analyze
4. Improve
5. Control

Each phase of the model has suggested tools and strategies to move from one phase to the next.

Sometimes, there are activities the *Leaner* Practitioner might want to perform before starting the DMAIC process. These include, but are not limited to, working with a smaller model such as PDCA or organizing the work space by using a 5S model.

A few recent examples of companies using the DMAIC model successfully in the workplace include:

- 3M
- Amazon
- Bank of America
- Boeing
- General Electric
- Northrup Grumman
- Raytheon

The DMAIC model is a structure that can successfully identify a process improvement, provide solutions and sustain the improvement. It also prepares the workplace to have a methodical approach to collaborating and analyzing new ideas and innovation. *Leaner* suggests that even smaller process improvements can benefit by using DMAIC thinking. Some process improvements do not need to be rigorously taken through each step of the model in-depth. Some smaller process improvements can benefit from simply thinking through the various phases of the model.

Section II

The DMAIC Model

6

Define Overview

It is never wrong to do the right thing.

Mark Twain

DMAIC (<u>DEFINE</u>-MEASURE-ANALYZE-IMPROVE-CONTROL)

The DMAIC model is a structured and disciplined approach to process improvement. It consists of five phases discussed in the previous chapter. Each phase is linked logically to the previous phase as well as to the next phase. This chapter covers the basics of Define.

Technically, there are only two major rules in define. Rule One is that it is necessary to start with a Process Map outlining the actual current process. Rule Two is that the *Leaner* Practitioner should not leave Define without a project charter. But by far, the true objective is to work on the right thing. Sometimes, the right thing and/or the right direction for the company needs to be examined.

Albert Einstein said that if he had only an hour to solve a problem he would spend 55 minutes thinking about the problem and only five minutes on the solution. Whereas this is not the exact intention of the Define portion of the DMAIC model, it does represent the concept that a great deal of time in problem solving should be devoted to thinking about the problem itself. This may seem logical to the reader, however, we live in a reactive environment that often starts trying to solve the problem without truly understanding the problem statement.

Having a standard problem-solving model such as DMAIC is extremely helpful. It provides teams with a roadmap. But without first spending serious time understanding the problem and why it is important, the DMAIC model doesn't work properly. In the words of Lewis Carroll paraphrased from *Alice in Wonderland*, if the *Leaner* Practitioner doesn't know where they are going, any road will get them there.

ELEMENTS OF DEFINE (DMAIC)

The tools most commonly used in the *Define* phase are:

- Project Charter
- Stakeholder Analysis
- High Level Process Mapping
- Suppliers, Inputs, Process, Output and Customers (SIPOC)
- Voice of the Customer (VOC)
- Value Stream Mapping
- Affinity Diagram
- Kano Model
- Critical-to-Quality (CTQ) Tree

The first phase is *Define*. During the *Define* phase, a team and its sponsors reach agreement on what the project is and what it should accomplish. Presuming that a draft of the Project Charter is already in place, the main work in the *Define* phase is for the project team to complete an analysis of what the project should accomplish and confirm understanding with the sponsor(s). They should agree on the problem, which customers are affected and how the current process or outcomes fail to meet their customers' needs through "Voice of the Customer (VOC) or Critical-to-Quality (CTQ)." The outcome of the *Define* phase is:

- A clear statement of the intended improvement (Project Charter)
- A high-level map of the processes (SIPOC)
- A list of what is important to the customer (CTQ)
- An understanding of the project's link to corporate strategy and its contribution to ROIC. The following sections provide a brief description of the above tools and techniques.

PROJECT CHARTER

The charter is a contract between the organization's leadership and the project team created at the outset of the project. Its purpose is:

- To set a clear definition of what the project is and is not
- To provide the parameters of the project
- A communication tool to align Sponsors, Champions and Teams
- To keep the project and team aligned with organizational priorities

STAKEHOLDER ANALYSIS

A DMAIC project will require a fundamental change in the process. To mitigate the resistance to change when the improvement is implemented, it is crucial to identify the stakeholders early on and to develop a communication plan for each of them. Typical stakeholders include managers, people who work in the process under study, upstream and downstream departments, customers, suppliers and finance. Regular communication can create more buy-in, identify better solutions and avoid pitfalls.

HIGH-LEVEL PROCESS MAP

A high-level process map is drawn to bring clarity to the project definition so the team members of the project understand what they are working toward.

SIPOC PROCESS MAP

A SIPOC is a high-level process map that includes Suppliers, Inputs, Process, Output and Customers. Quality is judged based on the output of a process. The quality is improved by analyzing inputs and process variables. An example of a SIPOC Process Map is provided below (Figure 6.1).

Feed the dog

Suppliers	Inputs	Process	Outputs	Customers
Grocery Store	• Go shopping • Buy dogfood • Return home • Put groceries away in cupboard	• Open cupboard • Get bowl • Fill bowl • Call dog	• Dog eats • Dog fertilizes garden	• Dog • Family • Garden

FIGURE 6.1
SIPOC process map example.

VOICE OF THE CUSTOMER

The VOC is a process used to capture the requirements/feedback from the customer (internal or external) to provide them with best-in-class service/product quality. This process is all about responsiveness and constantly innovating to capture the changing requirements of the customers over time.

The VOC is the term used to describe the stated and unstated needs or requirements of the customer. The VOC can be captured in a variety of ways:

- Direct discussion or interviews, surveys, focus groups, customer specifications, observation, warranty data, field reports and complaint logs
- These data are used to identify the quality attributes needed for a supplied component or material to incorporate in the process or product. The VOC is critical for an organization to:
- Decide what products and services to offer
- Identify critical features and specifications for those products and services

- Decide where to focus improvement efforts
- Obtain a baseline measure of customer satisfaction against which improvement will be measured
- Identify key drivers of customer satisfaction

IMPORTANT: *The larger the change, the more methods and tools should be used to collect an accurate and full picture of the voice of the customer. Additional insights can be gained from utilizing:*

- *Voice of the Employee (VOE)*
- *Voice of the Process (VOP)*
- *Voice of the Business (VOB)*

The following is a list of typical outputs of the VOC process:

- A list of customers and customer segments
- Identification of relevant reactive and proactive sources of data
- Verbal or numerical data that identify customer needs
- Defined Critical-to-Quality requirements (CTQs)
- Specifications for each CTQ requirement

AFFINITY DIAGRAM

An Affinity Diagram (sometimes referred to as a "KJ," after the initials of the person who created this technique, Kawakita Jiro) is a special kind of brainstorming tool. It is necessary to use an Affinity Diagram to:

- Gather large numbers of ideas, opinions or issues and group those items that are naturally related
- Identify, for each grouping, a single concept that ties the group together (Figure 6.2)

An Affinity Diagram is especially useful when:

- Chaos exists
- The team is drowning in a large volume of ideas

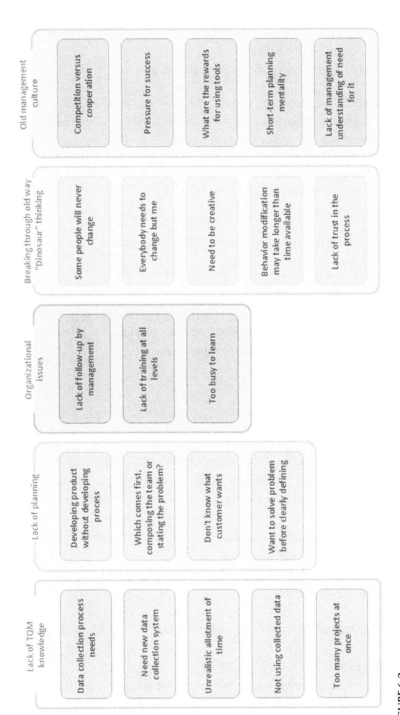

FIGURE 6.2
Affinity diagram example.

- Breakthrough thinking is required
- Broad issues or themes must be identified

Building an Affinity Diagram is a creative rather than a logical process.

KANO MODEL

Developed in the 1980s by Professor Noriaki Kano, the Kano model is based on the concepts of customer quality and provides a simple ranking scheme which distinguishes between essential and differentiating attributes. The model is a powerful way of visualizing product characteristics and stimulating debate within the design team. Kano also produced a rigorous methodology for mapping consumer responses into the model. Product characteristics can be classified as:

- **Threshold/Basic attributes**
  - Attributes which must be present for the product to be successful and can be viewed as a "price of entry." However, the customer will remain neutral toward the product even with improved execution of these threshold and basic attributes.
- **One-dimensional attribute** (Performance/Linear)
  - These characteristics are directly correlated to customer satisfaction. Increased functionality or quality of execution will result in increased customer satisfaction. Conversely, decreased functionality results in greater dissatisfaction. Product price is often related to these attributes.
- **Attractive attributes** (Exciters/Delighters)
  - Customers receive great satisfaction from a feature and are willing to pay a price premium. However, satisfaction will not decrease (below neutral) if the product lacks the feature. These features are often unexpected by customers and can be difficult to establish as needs during initial design. They are sometimes called unknown or latent needs.

An example of Kano model is provided below (Figure 6.3).

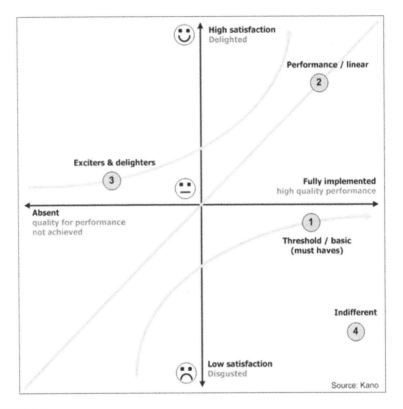

FIGURE 6.3
Kano model example.

CRITICAL-TO-QUALITY (CTQ) TREE

The purpose of Critical-to-Quality trees is to convert customer needs/ wants to measurable requirements for the business to implement.

For example: A retail merchant was receiving a significant number of complaints regarding their homeowner warranty policies from their customers. By analyzing customer survey data and developing the CTQ tree, the business was able to identify critical-to-satisfaction requirements. These requirements became the focus for improving customer satisfaction. The business eliminated mandatory warranty visits and made all warranty visits optional. Eliminating mandatory visits satisfied the customers who thought there were too many visits and adding an extra optional visit satisfied customers who thought there were too

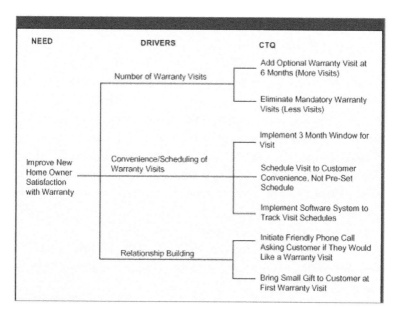

FIGURE 6.4
Needs-Drivers-CTQ

few visits. Expanding the time frame for scheduling warranty visits from 2 weeks to 3 months eliminated the inconvenience for customers who had busy schedules and found the time frame difficult to manage.

The business took a general, difficult-to-measure need (to improve home-owner warranty satisfaction) and developed specific, measurable and action-able requirements to drive improvements in customer satisfaction (Figure 6.4). In summary, the *Define* phase promotes identifying the true process improvement. This may involve doing a root cause analysis. It is vital to identify exactly which existing process is being explored in the hopes of making that process better, faster or more cost effective and be able to explain. In this phase, making sure the customer's requirements or CTQs are being met is what describes overall success in Lean Six Sigma. Therefore, listing to the VOC is crucial.

What is necessary to aim to make better, faster and more cost effective becomes the "Y" statement. *Define* is a creative phase and only two hard and fast rules exist. Rule One, it is necessary to create a high-level process map of the current condition. And, again, Rule Two is that the *Leaner* Practitioner should not leave *Define* without a project charter. There are, however, several tools available to get from a High-Level Process Map to the Project Charter.

The best approach to using defined in the workplace is to make sure the following are in place:

- Create or utilize a simple Project Charter form that is intuitive and easy to use.
- Explain the importance of a high-level current process map and do not overcomplicate the map for the mapping process.
- Deliver employee training that explains the difference between a problem statement and a "Y" statement. Remembering to point out that a problem statement can relate to any type of project, where as a "Y" statement is specific to the process improvement that needs to be better, faster or more cost effective.
- Ensure everyone involved in the process has a high-level understanding of the goals and objectives of the process improvement.

Albert Einstein, famous for many process improvement ideas, in one of his most well-known quotes states: "We cannot solve our problems with the same thinking we used when we created them." This is applicable to the *Define* phase of the DMAIC model. *Define* is a creative phase. It is a phase to ensure the right problem is being examined and creates an atmosphere of innovation to forward. It looks at those entities who will be most positively affected by the impact. It emphasizes inclusiveness and communication. It creates a structure to do the right thing and tackle the right problem that needs to be solved.

7

Measure Overview

Measurement is the first step that leads to control and eventually to improvement if you can't measure something you can't understand it if you can't understand it, you can't control it if you can't control it, you can't improve it.

H. James Harrington

DMAIC (DEFINE-<u>MEASURE</u>-ANALYZE-IMPROVE-CONTROL)

It is tempting not to pay attention to the current and skip ahead to solving the problem. Although Define offers the *Leaner* Practitioner a lot of information about what is happening now, the purpose of *Measure* is to take a more in-depth look. Albert Einstein said, "We cannot solve our problems with the same level of thinking that created them." Therefore, what is happening now, in real time, becomes very important. For example, what is working currently and what is not?

If it is possible to take a picture or a video, then do that! Before and after pictures are very powerful. A detailed process map may be just as good as taking a photograph. However, often a process map cannot accurately represent a picture. Therefore, the tools in *Measure* are important. For example, a picture or a video clip of how it is necessary to wash your clothes, now, might make a good reflection of what is happening, now, in current time. But, what if it is necessary to explain existing budgeting process? That might be more difficult. Remember, the purpose of the *Measure* phase is to give a true and accurate picture of the current condition as it relates to the project.

How the data will be collected is also something that should be considered. In this heightened age of both confidentiality and cyber security, a documented and endorsed plan should be in place before data are collected.

Most Lean Six Sigma professionals will agree that in order to document and collect data, the following things should be considered:

- Select the Critical-to-Quality (CTQ) characteristics in the necessary process. These are the outcomes of the given process that are important to the customer
- Determine what that process output should be, which is done by looking at the customer requirements and the project goal
- Describe the defects in the process. Remember, a defect is an outcome that falls outside the limits of customer's requirements or expectations and must be measurable
- Find the inputs to the process that contribute to defects
- Define an accurate dollar impact of eliminating the defects in terms of increased profitability and/or cost savings
- Measure the defects that affect the CTQ characteristics as well as any related factors
- Incorporate Measurement Systems Analysis—a method to make sure the defects are being measured properly
- Refine data collection procedures, if needed

Leaner theory would advocate exploring if any of the information, mentioned in the bullet points above, is already available. This data might be helpful even if it is fragmented or in draft form. It could save the *Leaner* Practitioner valuable time. In the *Leaner* world, it is important to determine the objective before identifying the tool. It is tempting to go through a checklist of tools in order to document work is being accomplished. However, using all existing materials contributes to making the process faster.

Leaner suggests using the following tools in *Measure* phase. These tools require that an intent or purpose be established first:

- Prioritization Matrix
- Process Cycle Efficiency
- Time Value Analysis
- Pareto Charts
- Control Charts
- Run Charts
- Failure Modes and Effect Analysis (FMEA)

Supporters of the Six Sigma only philosophy will mention the methodology's *demand* for a fact-based and data-driven analytical approach. This is, indeed, important. Lean supports this basic premise but softens the requirements and is a fan of simplification. *Leaner* would agree with both approaches as long as the concepts were made easier.

Leaner simply states that *all* the above-mentioned tools are not necessary for every project. In order to accomplish the mission quickly, a *Leaner* Practitioner considers which tools are the most meaningful to the project.

Consideration should also be given to which tools the *Leaner* Practitioner feels comfortable using and understands. If the *Leaner* Practitioner spends too much time learning the tool then it isn't particularly Lean.

Many improvement methodologies attempt process improvement without enough data to understand the underlying causes of the problem. Although *Analyze* is dedicated to a more thorough study as to why a condition is occurring, *Leaner* believes that thinking about why the problem is occurring just saves time down the line. Still, it is important not to develop a bias too early in the solution stage and to examine or measure as the DMAIC model prefers to say, all the conditions that are meaningful to solving the problem.

One of the goals of *Measure* is to tag the location or source of a problem. This makes the job in *Analyze* a little easier. Another important part of *Measure* is to establish baseline capability levels. Some capability awareness should have already happened in the *Define* phase. This is because if the process isn't capable (or does not have the capacity) of handling the process improvement, the *Leaner* Practitioner needs to deal with that issue before moving forward. However, baselines, standards and what is considered "the norm" are more aptly determined and documented in *Measure* phase.

Here is a summary of how the *Leaner* Practitioner would explain some of the core tools in *Measure*.

PRIORITIZATION MATRIX

The Prioritization Matrix provides a way of sorting a diverse set of items into an order of importance. This Matrix may also be used in other phases such as *Analyze* and *Improve*. It also enables their *relative* importance to be identified by deriving a numerical value of the importance of each item. Therefore, an item with a score of 223 is clearly far more important than one with a score of 23, but is not much more important than one with a

Health care problems

Problems	Frequency	Importance	Feasibility	Total points
1. No appointments for the afternoon	5	0	0	5
2. Delays in registration	6	1	5	12
3. Incomplete laboratory	9	11	6	26
4. Insufficient care in dentistry	10	12	8	30
5. Not enough doctors	6	0	5	11
6. Segregation of patients	7	11	11	29
7. Broken down ambulance	0	5	0	5
8. Not enough materials for the lab	3	0	0	3
9. Long waiting time	7	14	15	36
10. Disrespect of patients	4	7	10	21

FIGURE 7.1
Prioritization matrix.

score of 219. Items are compared, scored against a set of key criteria and the scores for each item are then summed (Figure 7.1).

PROCESS CYCLE EFFICIENCY

This is a calculation that relates the amount of value-added time to total cycle time in a process.

TIME VALUE ANALYSIS

This is a chart that visually separates value-added from non-value-added time in a process.

PARETO CHARTS

Vilfredo Pareto, a turn-of-the-century Italian economist, studied the distributions of wealth in different countries, concluding that a consistent minority—about 20%—of people controlled the large

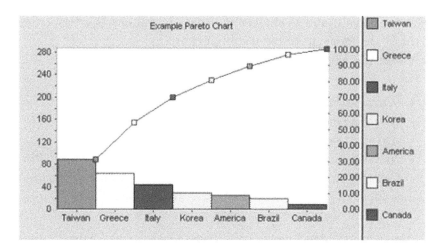

FIGURE 7.2
Example of a Pareto chart.

majority—about 80%—of a society's wealth. This same distribution has been observed in other areas and has been termed the Pareto effect (Figure 7.2).

The Pareto effect even operates in quality improvement: 80% of problems usually stem from 20% of the causes. Pareto charts are used to display the Pareto principle in action, arranging data so that the few vital factors that are causing most of the problems reveal themselves. Concentrating improvement efforts on these few issues will have a greater impact and be more cost effective than undirected efforts.

MEASUREMENT SYSTEMS ANALYSIS

A Measurement Systems Analysis, abbreviated MSA, is a specially designed experiment that seeks to identify the components of variation in the measurement. Just as processes that produce a product may vary, the process of obtaining measurements and data may have variation and produce defects. A Measurement Systems Analysis evaluates the test method, measuring instruments and the entire process of obtaining measurements to ensure the integrity of data used for analysis (usually quality analysis) and to understand the implications of measurement error for decisions made about a product or process.

A Measurement Systems Analysis considers the following:

- Selecting the correct measurement and approach
- Assessing the measuring device
- Assessing procedures & operators
- Assessing any measurement interactions
- Calculating the measurement uncertainty of individual measurement devices and/or measurement systems

Common tools and techniques of Measurement Systems Analysis include: calibration studies, fixed effect ANOVA, components of variance, Attribute Gage Study, Gage R&R, ANOVA Gage R&R, Destructive Testing Analysis and others. The tool selected is usually determined by characteristics of the measurement system itself.

A very popular MSA is Gage R&R. Gage Repeatability and Reproducibility is the amount of measurement variation introduced by a measurement system, which consists of the measuring instrument itself and the individuals using the instrument. A Gage R&R study quantifies three things:

1. Repeatability—variation from the measurement instrument
2. Reproducibility—variation from the individuals using the instrument
3. Overall Gage R&R, which is the combined effect of (1) and (2)

    In the case of a furniture manufacturing company, the project team performs a Gage R&R(GR&R) study on a known critical measurement (screw torque) that affects a cracking condition on one of its chair lines—this will come in handy later in the project. The initial Gage R&R results show that the screw torque measurement method introduces far too much variation.
4. Using a graphical technique learned in Gage R&R training, the team finds that the first operator in the study is recording consistently higher readings than the other two operators
5. Finally, after correcting operator #1's measurement technique and updating the measurement procedure, the team conducts a follow-up Gage R&R study with much-improved results.

CONTROL CHARTS

Every process varies. If it is necessary to write one's name ten times, the signatures will all be similar, but no two signatures will be exactly alike. There is an inherent variation, but it varies between predictable limits. If, during this process, someone bumps the elbow, it can result in an unusual variation due to what is called a "special cause." If, while cutting diamonds, someone bumps the elbow, the special cause can be expensive. For many processes, it is important to notice special causes of variation as soon as they occur.

There's also "common cause" variation. Consider a baseball pitcher. If he has good control, most of his pitches are going to be where he wants them. There will be some variation, but not too much. If he is "wild," his pitches aren't going where he wants them, there's more variation. There may not be any special causes—no wind, no change in the ball—just more "common cause" variation. The result: More walks are issued and there are unintended pitches over the plate where batters can hit them. In baseball, control wins ball games. Likewise, in most processes, reducing common cause variation saves money.

Happily, there are easy-to-use charts which make it easy see both special and common cause variations in a process. They are called control charts or sometimes Shewhart charts, after their inventor, Walter Shewhart, of Bell Labs. There are many different subspecies of control charts which can be applied to the different types of process data that are typically available (Figure 7.3).

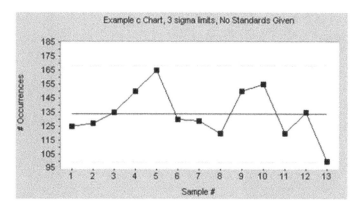

FIGURE 7.3
Example control chart.

All control charts have three basic components:

- A center line, usually the mathematical average of all the samples plotted
- Upper and lower statistical control limits that define the constraints of common cause variations
- Performance data plotted over time

RUN CHARTS

Run charts (often known as line graphs outside the quality management field) display process performance over time. Upward and downward trends, cycles and large aberrations may be spotted and investigated further. In a run chart, events, shown on the y axis, are graphed against a time period on the x axis. For example, a run chart in a hospital might plot the number of patient transfer delays against the time of day or day of the week. The results might show that there are more delays at noon than at 3 p.m. Investigating this phenomenon could unearth potential improvement needs. Run charts can also be used to track improvements that have been put into place, checking to determine their success. Also, an average line can be added to a run chart to clarify movement of the data away from the average (Figure 7.4).

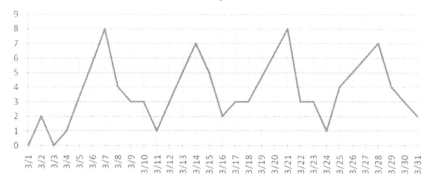

FIGURE 7.4
Example run chart.

FAILURE MODES AND EFFECT ANALYSIS (FMEA)

Procedures and tools that help to identify every possible failure mode of a process or product determine its effect on other sub-items and on the required function of the product or process. The FMEA is also used to rank & prioritize the possible causes of failure as well as develop and implement preventive actions, with responsible persons assigned to carry out these actions.

The purpose of *Measure* is to get a clear as-is idea of what is happening now. Take a picture if possible. Try a detailed process map. If it is still unclear what is going on in real time, try a simple tool, observation. It is always amazing how much can be learned by simply watching. The BEFORE picture is very important. Later, when the process improvement is rolled out, it will be the AFTER picture. Before-and-After pictures are the way to document the improvement. The other tools covered in this chapter help to do that as well.

Avoid these common mistakes:

- Measuring everything! Focus instead on a few critical measurements
- Forgetting to explain to employees why the data is needed and how it will be captured
- Collecting data that may not be useful to the project

To briefly summarize the *Measure* phase of the DMAIC model, it is where valid and reliable metrics are gathered to demonstrate a clear as-is picture of where the process is today. Later, when the process is improved, *Measure* will be used as the "before" picture.

The theory being that a problem can't really be solved without knowing what is going on in the 'Here and Now'. Understanding the dynamics of what is happening related to the process helps determine a solution.

The hardest part of *Measure* is gathering the information in a non-biased non-judgmental way. As much as possible, only the facts need to be recorded. In the next phase, *Analyze*, this information is evaluated. *Measure* is the "what" is happening now, whereas *Analyze* is the phase that questions "why" is that happening. In many cases, once the *Leaner* Practitioner truly understands the current dynamics a solution is either intuitive or obvious. This is another reason *Measure* is so valuable.

In the *Measure* phase common workplace uses include:

- Creating a detailed process map
- Compiling a data collection plan
- Understanding precisely what is happening now with a process that aims to be improved

The important thing to remember about the *Measure* phase is that without a clear concise picture of the current state, it may be difficult later to show a process improvement. Good process improvements happen almost behind the scenes. The idea is to make the process improvement without disrupting the workforce, but still get credit for the improvement that is been made.

Carlton Cuse is attributed with the same:

> "The creative process is not like a situation where you get struck by a single lightning bolt. You have ongoing discoveries, and there's ongoing creative revelations. Yes, it's helpful to be marching toward a specific destination, but, along the way, you must allow yourself room for your ideas to blossom, take root and grow." *Leaner* believes this is impossible to do without understanding everything that is going on now related to the process improvement project.

8

Analyze Overview

Without a Standard, there is no logical basis for decision-making or taking action.

Joseph Juran

DMAIC (DEFINE-MEASURE-ANALYZE-IMPROVE-CONTROL)

Performed correctly, *Measure* has identified and documented the current process. What is happening now, in relationship to, the activity that needs to be improved? Now, it's time to analyze that picture. Sometimes being made aware of "what's happening now" will lead the *Leaner* Practitioner to an automatic solution. Other times, it will be necessary to do a deeper analysis. The end goal of *Analyze* is to present 3–5 solutions that will make the current process better, faster or more cost effective. It is important to remember that one of the solutions may be, do nothing.

Steve Maraboli stated: "Sometimes problems don't require a solution to solve them; instead they require maturity to outgrow them."

In the *Analyze* phase of the DMAIC model, the root cause of the current condition is explored along with correlation, impact and variation. This examination should lead to a list of possible solutions.

Sun Tzu, in *The Art of War*, makes an interesting observation. There are only a handful of musical notes. And, yet, the combinations, of these notes, produce more melodies than can ever be heard. This implies that there is an infinite number of outcomes to any effort.

The *Analyze* phase can be approached by using a series of questions:

1. What are the perceived causes of the process variability and which can we control?
2. What is of value to the customer?
3. What are the detail steps of the process?
4. Have the "As-Is" causes been validated?

The tools most commonly used in the *Analyze* phase are:

- Brainstorming
- Cause and Effect Diagram
- Affinity Diagrams (covered in the *Define* phase)
- Control Charts (covered in the *Measure* phase)
- Flow Diagram
- Pareto Charts (covered in the *Measure* phase)
- Regression Analysis
- Scatter Plots

This is a summary of how most professionals, if given only a short time to explain, would explain the above tools.

5 WHYS ANALYSIS

The 5 Whys Analysis is a problem-solving technique that allows *Leaner* Practitioner to get at the root cause of a problem quickly. It was made popular as part of the Toyota Production System (1970s). Application of the strategy involves taking any problem and asking "Why—what caused this problem?"

By repeatedly asking the question "Why" (five is a good rule), it is possible to peel away the layers of symptoms to identify the root cause of a problem. Very often the first reason for a problem will lead to another question and then to another. Although this technique is called "5 Whys," it might be necessary to ask the question fewer or more times than five before the issue related to a problem is found.

KEY CONCEPT

Benefits of the 5 Whys:

- It helps to quickly identify the root cause of a problem.
- It helps determine the relationship between different root causes of a problem.
- It can be learned quickly and doesn't require statistical analysis to be used.

Here is an example of the 5 Why thinking process:

1. Why is our largest customer unhappy? Because our deliveries of bicycles have been late for the last month.
2. Why have our bicycle deliveries been late for the last month? Because production has been behind schedule.
3. Why has production been behind schedule? Because there is a shortage of wheels.
4. Why are we having a shortage of wheels? Because incoming inspection has rejected many wheels for not being round.
5. Why are we rejecting so many parts? Because purchasing switched to a cheaper wheel supplier that has inconsistent quality.

BRAINSTORMING

Brainstorming is simply listing all ideas put forth by a group in response to a given problem or question. In 1939, a team led by advertising executive Alex Osborn coined the term "brainstorm." According to Osborn, "Brainstorming a group problem-solving techniques that involving the spontaneous contribution of ideas from all members of the group" Creativity is encouraged by not allowing ideas to be evaluated or discussed until everyone had the chance to contribute. All ideas are considered worthy. Sometimes, it is the most unlikely thought, that renders a good solution. Even though brainstorming is a popular procedure many facilitators forget the basics. The collection of data should be captured without bias.

Done right, it taps the human brain's capacity for lateral thinking and free association.

Brainstorms help answer specific questions such as:

- What opportunities face us this year?
- What factors are constraining performances in Department X?
- What could be causing problem Y?
- What can we do to solve problem Z?

Brainstorming can help positively identify causes of problems, rank ideas in a meaningful order, select important ideas or check solutions.

CAUSE & EFFECT (C&E) DIAGRAM

The Cause & Effect diagram is the brainchild of Kaoru Ishikawa, who pioneered quality management processes in the Kawasaki shipyards and, in the process, became one of the founding fathers of modern management. C&E diagrams are also called Ishikawa diagrams or fishbone diagrams. The C&E diagram is used to explore all the potential or real causes (or inputs) that result in a single effect (or output). Causes are arranged according to their level of importance or detail, resulting in a depiction of relationships and hierarchy of events. This can help to search for root causes, identify areas where there may be problems and compare the relative importance of different causes.

Causes in a C&E diagram are frequently arranged into four major categories. While these categories can be anything, one will often see:

- Manpower, methods, materials and machinery (recommended for manufacturing)
- Policies, procedures and people (recommended for administration and service)

These guidelines can be helpful, but should not be used if they limit the diagram or are inappropriate. The categories chosen to use should suit

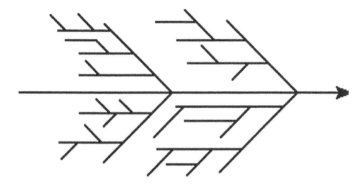

FIGURE 8.1
Example Simple Fishbone Structure.

specific needs. Often, we can create the branches of the cause and effect tree from the titles of the affinity sets in a preceding affinity diagram.

The C&E diagram is also known as the fishbone diagram because it is drawn to resemble the skeleton of a fish, with the main causal categories drawn as "bones" attached to the spine of the fish (Figure 8.1).

FLOW DIAGRAMS

Flowcharts are maps or graphical representations of a process. Steps in a process are shown with symbolic shapes and the flow of the process is indicated with arrows connecting the symbols. Computer programmers popularized flowcharts in the 1960s, using them to map the logic of programs. In quality improvement work, flowcharts are particularly useful for displaying how a process currently functions or could ideally function. Flowcharts can help the *Leaner* Practitioner see whether the steps of a process are logical, uncover problems or miscommunications, define the boundaries of a process and develop a common base of knowledge about a process. Flowcharting a process often brings to light redundancies, delays, dead ends and indirect paths that would otherwise remain unnoticed or ignored. But flowcharts don't work if they aren't accurate, if team members are afraid to describe what happens or if the team is too far removed from the actual workings of the process.

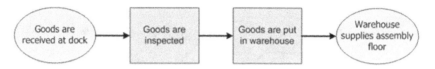

FIGURE 8.2
High-level flow diagram example.

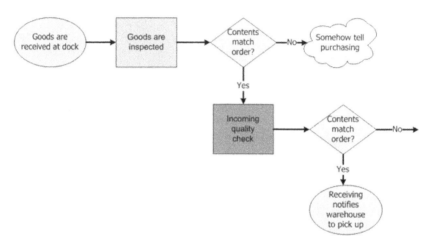

FIGURE 8.3
Detailed flow diagram example.

There are many flowchart symbols that may be used. Experience has shown that there are three main types that work for almost all situations.

High-level flowcharts only map the major steps in a process and provide a good overview (Figure 8.2).

Detailed flowcharts show a step-by-step mapping of all events and decisions in a process (Figure 8.3).

Deployment flowcharts, also referred to as Swim Lane charts organize the flowchart by columns with each column representing a person or department involved in a process (Figure 8.4).

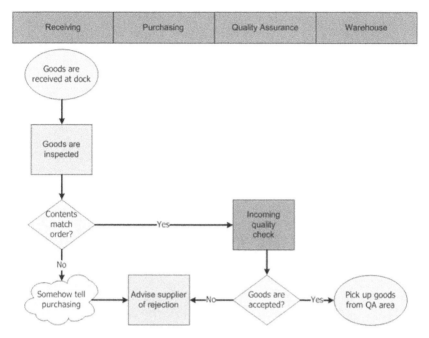

FIGURE 8.4
Deployment flow diagram/swim lane chart example.

REGRESSION ANALYSIS

Regression analysis is a statistical forecasting model that describes and evaluates the relationship between a given variable, usually called the dependent variable and one or more other variables, usually known as the independent variables. Regression analysis models are used to help us predict the value of one variable compared to one or more other variables whose values can be predetermined.

SCATTER PLOTS

Scatter Plots (also called scatter diagrams) are used to investigate the possible relationship between two variables that both relate to the same "event." A straight line of best fit, using the least squares method, is often included (Figure 8.5).

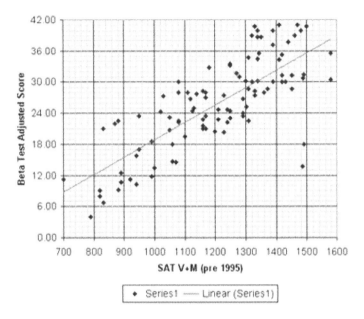

FIGURE 8.5
Scatter plot example.

Things to look for in a scatter plot:

- If the points cluster in a band running from lower left to upper right, there is a positive correlation (if x increases, y increases)
- If the points cluster in a band from upper left to lower right, there is a negative correlation (if x increases, y decreases)
- Imagine drawing a straight line or curve through the data so that they "fit" as well as possible. The more the points cluster closely around the imaginary line of best fit, the stronger the relationship that exists between the two variables

If it is hard to see where it is necessary would draw a line and if the points show no significant clustering, there is probably no correlation (Figure 8.6).

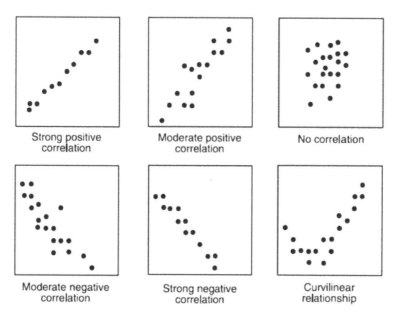

FIGURE 8.6
Correlation patterns.

VARIATION

See the following model to get a better idea of Variation (Figure 8.7). These topics are covered in most LSS Black Belt programs. Here is a quick graphic to get a better understanding:

The *Analyze* phase is where most traditional Lean Six Sigma and Six Sigma classes spend their time in instructing the student. In Six Sigma, this is also where statistics are discussed.

Often, especially in Lean Six Sigma projects, statistics are not as useful because there are not enough data points. Using math and statistics can be useful in *Analyze* phase, but not always necessary to the extent they are used.

Another thing to remember about this phase is that the *Leaner* Practitioner doesn't want to end up with more than 3–5 solutions because too many or not enough choices can be confusing.

Analyze (the third phase of the DMAIC model) is where the information from the *Measure* phase is evaluated. Identifying and eliminating

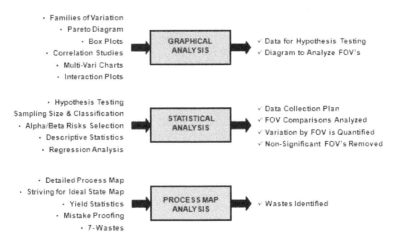

FIGURE 8.7
Types of variation.

variation could result in an automatic process improvement. Other lenses the data should be examined through include:

- Root Causes
- Correlation
- Impact

These conditions are reviewed and analyzed for the purpose of coming up with 3–5 solutions. There are other considerations when determining these solutions based on information gathered in the *Define* and *Measure* phases. For example, during *Define* and/or *Measure* phases the *Leaner* Practitioner may have discovered additional information such as budget, constraints, obstacles or political considerations. Any knowledge gathered in the previous two phases will be valuable in the *Analyze* phase when determining which solutions should be presented in the next phase, *Improve*.

Before analyzing data, it is important to clearly understand the current state. It is equally important that the data are validated. The type of data should also be considered. Quantitative data are information about quantities. To simplify, it is information that can be written down and expressed with numbers. Examples of quantitative data are things such as height for the length of a fingernails.

Qualitative deals with data that can be observed, for example, sight, smell, touch and taste, it does not involve measurement or numbers. For example, colors and shapes are examples of qualitative data. Qualitative data are extremely varied in nature, they include almost any information that can be captured that's not numerical.

It seems obvious why quantitative data are so important in data analysis. However, the purpose of qualitative data is sometimes confusing. When considering qualitative data think of information to be gained from observation from one-on-one interviews and from conducting focus groups. Although this information is not numerical, it is valuable in problem-solving. In other words, any information acquired that cannot be captured numerically is qualitative data.

In the workplace, there are many areas that use data analysis other than process improvement. Still, what is being analyzed is often related to the root cause, correlation, impact and variation. Some specific examples in the workplace after collecting the data (the *Measure* phase) include:

- Organizing the data into graphs and charts that make the data easier to understand
- Scrutinizing and studying the data to create a list of 3–5 solutions that could make the current process better, faster and more cost effective
- Documenting the logic behind each possible solution

The true purpose of the *Analyze* phase is to form the logical foundation for the 3–5 solutions.

9

Improve Overview

All improvement happens project by project and in no other way.

Joseph Juran

DMAIC (DEFINE-MEASURE-ANALYZE-IMPROVE-CONTROL)

The *Improve* phase has many facets. It is where most of the solution time will be spent in the DMAIC model. But an easier way to think about *Improve* is that it provides an opportunity to mistake-proof the process improvement solution before rolling out the actual project.

Improve works first to gain consensus. Which of the 3–5 solutions from *Analyze* should be tried? How will the idea be piloted or tried out? Then, after these questions are answered, a project plan is created and rolled out.

Gaining consensus, as to which solution should be tried, creates buy-in. Alvin Toffler, an associate editor for *Fortune* magazine said, "It is always easier to talk about change than to make it." Creating true buy-in helps with the impending change. Process improvement always represents changing something. Lean Six Sigma and *Leaner* support the concept that people factors are the primary make-or-break considerations leading to a successful project.

The *Leaner* Practitioner understands that Improve is basically a road-map. It does not have the creativity found in the previous three phases: Define–Measure–Analyze. Once the *Leaner* Practitioner is in the *Improve* phase it is important to follow these precise activities:

- Present the 3-5 solutions recorded at the end of the *Analyze* phase
- Gain Consensus
- Try out the solution—if it works move forward, if not choose another solution from the list
- Create the project plan
- Execute the project plan
- Move to the *Control* phase if an improvement can be documented

Much of this chapter is dedicated to project management. Once a solution is selected, Improve is mostly about basic Project Management. The basics of Project Management defining the problem solution (which is what the DMAIC helps one do), building a project plan, executing that plan and managing resources to meet the project baseline. The project baseline is what is determined your project will cost (cost baseline) and how long it will take (time baseline).

Tools used in the *Improve* phase, that have already been used in other phases of the DMAIC include:

- Brainstorming
- Flowcharting
- FMEA
- Stakeholder Analysis
- 5S Method

There are also more sophisticated tools used in Improve should the project be more robust in nature and need additional assistance. A brief explanation will follow. These tools include, but are not limited to:

- Setup Reduction
- Queuing Methods for Reducing Congestion and Delay
- Kaizen

SETUP REDUCTION

Key Concept

The benefits of Setup Reduction:

- Reduce lead time, resulting in improved delivery
- Improve documentation of setup processes, leading to improved processes
- Decreased inventory and costs, while increasing capacity

Setup reduction is the process of reducing changeover time (i.e., from the last good piece of the previous run to the first good piece of the next run). Since setup activities add no marketable form, fit or function to the product, they are non-value adding. The tool for tackling setup time is the Four-Step Rapid Setup method. The principle of this method is to eliminate anything that interrupts or hinders productivity. The following steps provide a high-level description of the *Four-Step Rapid Setup method*:

Step #1—Identify and tabulate any process-related activity that fits into one or more of the following categories:
- Activity that delays the start of value-added work
- Activity that causes interruptions to value-added work
- Activity where it is similar or identical to another task in the process

Step #2—See if any of the interruptive/delaying tasks can be offloaded: Our focus here is to move preparatory work outside of the main process flow so that information or material ends up waiting for the person, not the other way around. The goal is to quickly complete value-added work without any non-value-added activity.

Step #3—Streamline or automate any interruptive/delaying tasks that cannot be offloaded.

Step #4—Bring the process under statistical control: The setup is not complete until the output of the process is "within specification" and under statistical control, meaning the amount of variation in lead time is within predictable limits of $+/- 3$ sigma.

Queuing Methods for Reducing Congestion and Delays

Often congestion occurs because of variation in demand, much like travel congestion and delays that we all witness during the holiday season. Once identified, there are two principal techniques for reducing congestion that arises from variation in the demand for service.

- **Pooling**: Cross-training staff to step in during times of peak loads. One hotel chain, for example, trains their office and other staff to help with registration during unexpected and predictable peak times.
- **Triaging**: Sorting jobs into categories that reflect different levels of effort required.

Typical schemes include: Fast service times versus slow service times and routine problems versus catastrophic problems. Once Triaging categories have been identified, it is necessary to then develop different strategies to deal with each category.

KAIZEN

Kaizen is often translated in the West as ongoing, continuous improvement. Some authors explain Japan's competitive success in the world marketplace as the result of the implementation of the Kaizen concept in Japanese corporations. In contrast to the usual emphasis on evolutionary, innovative change on an occasional basis, Kaizen looks for uninterrupted, ongoing incremental change. In other words, there is always room for improvement and continuously trying to become better.

In practice, Kaizen can be implemented in corporations by improving every aspect of a business process in a step-by-step approach, while gradually developing employee skills through training and increased involvement. Principles in Kaizen implementation are:

- Human resources are the most important company asset
- Processes must evolve by gradual improvement rather than radical changes

Improvement must be based on statistical/quantitative evaluation of process performance. Remember Improve is a roadmap. Don't take a detour or the process is at risk! It is important to follow these steps summarized as:

- Choose the solution from the list the *Leaner* Practitioner developed in *Analyze*
- Get consensus
- Try it out
- Create a project plan
- Roll it out and stay in Improve until the *Leaner* Practitioner sees an improvement has been accomplished

Key among his or her duties is the recognition that risk directly impacts the likelihood of success and that this risk must be both formally and informally measured throughout the lifetime of the project.

Risks arise from uncertainty and the successful *Leaner* Practitioner is the one who focuses on this as the main concern. Most of the issues that impact a project arise in one way or another from risk. A good *Leaner* Practitioner lessens risk significantly, often by adhering to a policy of open communication, ensuring every significant participant has an opportunity to express opinions and concerns.

Every decision taken by the *Leaner* Practitioners should be taken in such a way that it directly benefits the project.

A *Leaner* Practitioner may use project management software, such as Microsoft Project, to organize their tasks and workforce. These software packages allow the *Leaner* Practitioner to produce reports and charts in a few minutes, compared with the several hours it can take if they do it by hand.

Roles and Responsibilities

The role of the *Leaner* Practitioner may include many of the following activities:

- Planning and Defining Scope
- Activity Planning and Sequencing
- Resource Planning
- Developing Schedules
- Time Estimating
- Cost Estimating
- Developing a Budget
- Documentation
- Creating Charts and Schedules

- Risk Analysis
- Managing Risks and Issues
- Monitoring and Reporting Progress
- Team Leadership
- Strategic Influencing
- Business Partnering
- Working with Vendors
- Scalability, Interoperability and Portability Analysis
- Controlling Quality
- Benefits Realization

The DMAIC model can align with these steps or the steps can be used prior to developing the actual project plan. The *Improve* phase involves creating a project plan. This requires a basic understanding of project management. Depending on the approach selected for the project, this knowledge can take on different characteristics and nuances. The following section on the 5 Basic Phases of Project Management is generally the most accepted.

Most agree that basic project management essentially has five steps.

Basic Phases of Traditional Project Management

Project Management Institute, Inc. defines project management as "The application of knowledge, skills, tools and techniques to a broad range of activities in order to meet the requirements of a particular project." The process of directing and controlling a project from start to finish may be further divided into five basic phases:

1. Project conception and initiation
   An idea for a project will be carefully examined to determine whether it benefits the organization. During this phase, a decision-making team will identify if the project can realistically be completed.
2. Project definition and planning
   A project plan, project charter and/or project scope may be put in writing, outlining the work to be performed. During this phase, a team should prioritize the project, calculate a budget and schedule and determine what resources are needed.
3. Project launch or execution
   Resources' tasks are distributed and teams are informed of responsibilities. This is a good time to bring up important project related information.

4. Project performance and control

Project Manager will compare project status and progress to the actual plan, as resources perform the scheduled work. During this phase, the Project Manager may need to adjust schedules or do what is necessary to keep the project on track.

5. Project close

After project tasks are completed and the client has approved the outcome, an evaluation is necessary to highlight project success and/or learn from project history.

Projects and project management processes vary from industry to industry, however, these are more traditional elements of a project. The overarching goal is typically to offer a product change a process or to solve a problem in order to benefit the organization.

The key activities in *Improve* involve choosing a solution and implementing a solid project plan. The *Leaner* Practitioner can continue to the next phase by ensuring a process improvement has been made. The way the manager knows the improvement has been made is by comparing the Before Picture (the *Measure* phase) to the After Picture (the *Improve* phase).

It is important to use the same tools in *Measure* as those used in *Improve*. Again, a Before-and-After picture is the best documentation.

To summarize the *Improve* phase in the *Leaner* Six Sigma workshops presented by SSD Global Solutions, we often mention that *Improve* phase is basically a roadmap. *Define, Measure* and even *Analyze* are creative phases where the *Leaner* Practitioner is given suggestions and information on what should be defined, measured or analyzed. Once in the *Improve* phase it is about following the specific action steps:

Step One: Present the 3–5 solutions that would make the process in question better, faster or more cost effective

Step Two: Gain consensus

Step Three: Conduct a pilot

Step Four: If the pilot is successful, create a project plan. If the pilot is not successful, choose another solution from Step One

Step Five: Execute the project plan

The *Leaner* Practitioner stays in Step Five until some improvement has been realized. This is demonstrated by comparing the picture in *Improve* to the picture in *Measure*—essentially looking at a before and after picture.

The process does not have to be completely improved for the *Leaner* Practitioner to begin activities in the *Control* phase.

The most common activities that occur in the *Improve* phase are as follows:

- Consensus gathering
- Piloting
- Designing and executing the project plan
- Verifying the solution is working

Activities in the *Improve* phase include:

- Gaining consensus and tools related to facilitation to accomplish consensus
- Building a project management plan in work breakdown structure (WBS)
- Mistake-proofing the project plan

Mark Twain said, "Continuous Improvement is better than delayed perfection." The *Improve* phase of the DMAIC model is about making the best decision based on the information gathered from the *Define*, *Improve* and *Analyze* phases. Then, acting on that decision by using a project plan. If the plan shows an effort toward improvement, the *Leaner* Practitioner has met the goal of the *Improve* phase.

10

Control Overview

Coming together is a beginning. Keeping together is progress. Working together is Success.

Henry Ford

DMAIC (DEFINE-MEASURE-ANALYZE-IMPROVE-CONTROL)

In the *Control* phase, the objective is to build a sustainability plan where everyone can successfully work together to maintain the improvement. Often people believe that something can be improved temporarily, but it won't stay that way. This causes a lack of buy-in. Why work on something that will just go back to the way it was? The effort feels fruitless. Therefore, building a plan that demonstrates how the process can be preserved is important to success.

The primary objective of this phase in the DMAIC model is to provide a simple plan that easily documents how to keep the improvement in place.

Much of *Control* has to do with the way the process improvement is documented. It is also about helping those involved in the process recognize red flags and letting them know the specific action that should be taken. Many times, if the instructions or documentation is too complicated or not made readily available, the suggestions won't be adopted. In order to sustain an improvement, it is necessary to produce checklists and/or assign individual responsibility to certain tasks.

The tools most commonly used in *Control* phase are:

- Control Charts
- Failure Mode Effect Analysis (FMEA) forms
- Transition Plans
- ROI Formulas

Control Charts

As a reminder, Control Charts are a statistical process control tool used to determine if the process is in a state of control. There are three main elements of a Control Chart:

1. A Control Chart begins with a time series graph.
2. A central line (X) is added as a visual reference for detecting shifts or trends – this is also referred to as the process location.
3. Upper and lower control limits (UCL and LCL) are computed from available data and placed equidistant from the central line. This is also referred to as process dispersion.

There are several names for these charts, but the two main categories are Control Charts for Variables and Control Charts for Attributes. Variable data is called discrete data in order to be counted or useful. Attribute data is qualitative data that can be counted for recording and analysis.

Variables are created with a name, type and shape before they are assigned data values, so a variable may exist with no values. The value of an attribute is specified when it is created, unless it is a zero-length attribute.

FMEA Forms

Failure Mode and Effects Analysis (FMEA) is a step-by-step approach for identifying all possible failures in a design, a manufacturing or assembly process or a product or service. It is a common process analysis tool.

The types of FMEA are

- System – focuses on global system functions.
- Design – focuses on components and subsystems.

- Process – focuses on manufacturing and assembly processes.
- Service – focuses on service functions.
- Software – focuses on software functions.

Forms that collect this information vary, depending on the industry and type, but most include:

- The task
- The severity if the task fails
- How often the task has failed in the past?
- How likely will detection be that the task is about to fail?
- Who oversees the task and/or who is monitoring/evaluating the task?

A common result of a FMEA is a Risk Priority Number or RPN. This number is assigned to tasks in a process. The *Leaner* Practitioner bases this numeric value on the following factors: likelihood of occurrence, likelihood of detection and severity of impact.

ROI Formulas

As a reminder, Return-on-Investment (ROI), is the ratio of a profit or loss made in a fiscal year expressed in terms of an investment and shown as a percentage of increase or decrease in the value of the investment during the year in question. The standard formula for ROI is:

$$ROI = Net\ Profit\ /\ Total\ Investment\ *\ 100.$$

In the initial project charter, a projected ROI is captured. This is the best guess at what the project, if successful, would make, save or avoid spending. It might be on factors such as demand in the workplace, cost of acquiring a new customer or the strategic plan. It could be based on experience or on a case study.

In the *Control* phase, since definitive results have been achieved, the standard ROI formula captures the information.

Quality Control

The ultimate purpose in Quality Control (QC) is overall assurance that a high standard of quality is met. The customer's expectations depend on this, so control is inherently associated with quality.

An important factor in Lean Six Sigma is to reduce defects. Therefore, QC is necessary along with mistake-proofing. QC is an essential method used to keep the process on track. It enables the *Leaner* Practitioner the ability to recognize an fix problems proactively. QC also determines facets of how well the project was executed and implemented.

Quality Control is the heart of Lean Six Sigma methodology. Naturally, the *Leaner* Practitioner understands that perfection is an ideal and rarely can be accomplished. However, making the effort defines the *Leaner* Practitioner's attitude.

Standardization

One feature of successful process improvement is to make sure the process flows easily. This usually means standardization. In manufacturing environment the value of standardization has been a proven concept for many years.

Standardization enables high quality production of goods and services on a reliable, predictable and sustainable basis. Standardization is making sure that important elements of a process are performed consistently in the most effective manner. Changes are made only when data show that a new alternative is better. Use of standard practices will:

- Reduce variation among individuals or groups and make process output more predictable
- Provide "know-why" for operators and managers now on the job
- Deliver a basis for training new employees
- Offer a path for tracing problems
- Offer a way to capture and retain knowledge

Responding When Defects Occur

The final step in any control process is knowing how to respond, once a defect is discovered. The weak links in the procedure, where defects are most likely to occur, should be monitored carefully.

At the end of the control process the *Leaner* Practitioner should determine a way to reward the team and stakeholders if possible. Rewards are usually contingent on the *Leaner* Practitioner's available budget. However, there are many creative low-cost ways to recognize the contributors to a project.

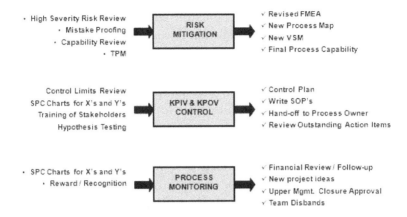

Control is about keeping the improvement in place. The opening statement in the *Control* phase, regardless if the *Leaner* Practitioner is doing a presentation or a written report, should reiterate what the problem was, what solution was chosen and what did it make, save or avoid the company from spending (ROI).

The next step is documenting the sustainability plan. This plan should be geared to the entity that will now be managing the project. The final step is to perform the close-out activities that would occur with any project. This would include things such as updating documentation, celebrating the success, publishing results and letting those involved know that this part of the project has been completed.

Summarizing *Control* is easy. There are three basic parts:

Part One: Articulate the benefits of the project in the terms of dollars saved, made or were avoided spending. Sometimes concessions must be made for the person reading the *Control* phase. It may be necessary to briefly explain what was done and its important.

Part Two: Document the sustainability plan. What controls need to be put in place to ensure the process improvement continues. This is an audience-based task. Someone who is knowledgeable about the process improvement may not need as much information as someone who is not, but has been assigned the task of keeping the process improvement in place.

If, for example, the *Leaner* Practitioner continues to manage the process improvement, a check sheet might suffice. And, with the simple process improvements, visual controls might be enough.

A formal transition plan puts the goals, priorities and strategies in place for a successful transition of your process. Without a clearly defined plan, *Leaner* Practitioners are leaving the future of their process improvement to chance.

A Control Plan is a method for documenting the functional elements of quality control that are to be implemented in order to assure that process improvement stays in place or is optimized. In some cases, companies have formal Control Plan templates. The intent of the Control Plan is to formalize and document the system of control that will be utilized. The *Leaner* Practitioner should check to see if this document is available. If it is, this collateral should be included, in narrative form, as a component of *Control*. The form itself should be completed, reference in *Control* and attached as an appendix to the DMAIC report. The elements of a formalized Control Plan describe the CTQs of the process improvement and how the process should be monitored or controlled moving forward.

Both the Transition Plan and Control Plan would appear or be referenced in this section should the *Leaner* Practitioner elect to use the document/s.

Part Three: Closing out the project. This part relies heavily on normal closeout procedures. Examples of closeout procedures include, but are not limited to, updating documents, best practices, celebrating the team or anyone involved and letting suppliers and other contributors know that the project is complete.

Many companies have a formal closeout procedure. If formal process or form is in place, it should be included or referenced in the *Control* phase. Like a formal Transition or Control Plan it may also be included as an appendix to the DMAIC report.

Project close-out should be anticipated and planned as early as possible in the project lifecycle even though it is often the last major process of a project's life. The primary tasks will focus on verifying the acceptance of the final deliverables. But often closeout also includes:

- Debriefing
- What was the outcome of this project?
- Team performance evaluation

- Lessons learned
- New team abilities as a result of the project?
- Updating documents
- Rewarding the team

Typically, in the workplace, activities in *Control* include:

- Documenting the benefit in the terms of dollars and cents
- Making a stainable plan to maintain the improvement
- Close out activities

The focus of the *Control* phase is to make sure that the action items created in the *Improve* phase are well-implemented and maintained.

Section III

Standards

11

The Impact of ISO Standard 13053: *Six Sigma on the* Leaner *Approach*

For the *Leaner* Practitioner who may be new to the International Organization for Standardization (ISO), it is important to review some basics about ISO standards before understanding the worldwide impact of ISO 13053 for Six Sigma.

ISO is a global federation of national standards bodies. ISO publishes several standards. Standards are requirements and/or best practices involved to improve an organization. Currently, there are over 300 standards available. Many standards offer organizations the ability to apply for ISO certification. Certification means that, according to an ISO auditor, the organization involved has met the requirements set forth in a specific standard. The work of preparing the standard is carried out through ISO technical committees. These committees include subject matter experts as well as ISO representatives. However, some standards are intended as guidelines and do not offer certification.

The best-known ISO standards in the United States belong to the ISO 9000 series. ISO 9001:2008 is the most commonly used standard in the United States. First published in 1987, ISO 9001 is the original management standard. This standard has been updated many times. The objective of the standard is to provide a framework to assess a company's ability to meet the needs of the customer. Simplified, this standard requires organizations to: (1) identify their quality management system (QMS) and (2) continually improve the QMS process. Entities must be registered with ISO to qualify for ISO certification.

Generally, the process of registration involves these steps:

- Application is made to a certified ISO registrar
- An assessment is made by the registrar involving two steps:
  - Readiness Survey
  - Quality Management System Review
- Registration may be granted or the organization may be required to perform a series of tasks prior to registration

Companies hire a consultant to prepare for registration. The consultant may be independent or be an employee of a certified ISO registrar. Internal audits may also be performed by a consultant prior to the official audit. Several companies elect to train a few employees to perform these mock audit activities either for the initial certification or for a re-certification effort. Re-certification timeframes are prescribed by the specific standard, but can also be contingent on how well compliance to the standard is being met.

Sometimes, ISO 9001:2008 is referred to as ISO 9000 because it is part of the ISO 9000 series. However, the document ISO 9000 is a supporting document related to fundamentals and vocabulary of the standard. Prior to the year 2000, there were separate ISO 9000 standards that governed companies responsible for making products in contrast to companies that handled only the distribution of products. These two standards, ISO 9002 and ISO 9003, are no longer supported. ISO 9004 is a guidance document that helps explain the requirements of ISO 9001:2008. If a specific section of the standard does not apply, an organization may request exclusion. The next revision of this standard is scheduled for release in 2015.

Many *Leaner* Practitioners already work with ISO 9001:2008 because the standard is suitable for all sizes and types of organizations, including hospitals and the healthcare industry. The *Leaner* Practitioner can reflect an accurate picture of an organization's current state as well as create viable measurement and tracking systems. These competencies are fundamental to the ISO certification process.

The primary goal of ISO 9001:2008 is to increase customer satisfaction. This is supported by better management controls and engaging in continuous process improvement. The *Leaner* Practitioner can impact this initiative by eliminating errors, reducing waste and providing sustainability models.

The second most recognized standard in the United States is ISO 14001. ISO 14001 focuses on how environmental issues are managed. First published in 1996, this standard supports the principles of ISO 9001:2008, but adds environmental considerations. Generally, there are four major stages to the certification process. These include:

- Environmental Review
- Environmental Policy Creation
- Documenting the Environmental Management System (EMS)
- Audit and Review

The *Leaner* Practitioner interested in working with ISO 14001 should be familiar with the environmental efforts of the company as well as any compliance issues for that specific industry and/or governmental regulations.

The introduction of ISO 13053 for Six Sigma is an exciting development for the *Leaner* Practitioner. Although the standard is specifically named Six Sigma, it contains many components typically associated with Lean Manufacturing, Continuous Improvement (CI) and Operational Excellence (OE). For the *Leaner* Practitioner, working in ISO 9000 or ISO 14000 environments, the Six Sigma standard adds another layer of credibility to process improvement.

Many Six Sigma professionals rely on the American Society of Quality (ASQ) Six Sigma Black Belt Body of Knowledge (ASQ-SSBOK). This document provides an outline of topics that should be understood for the ASQ Six Sigma Black Belt certification exam. Many topics listed in the ASQ-SSBOK are the same as those covered in ISO 13053. However, differences also are evident. For example, ASQ-SSBOK supports more references to the history and value of Six Sigma, leadership and the maturity of teams. ISO 13053 places more emphasis on tools, implementation and the maturity of an organization.

ISO 13053 is divided into two standards: ISO 13053-1 and ISO 13053-2. ISO 13053-1 covers the DMAIC methodology. ISO 13053-2 covers tools used in the DMAIC process.

ISO 13053-1

This part of ISO 13053 records the best practices that should be followed in each of the phases of the DMAIC model. It makes management recommendations and gives an overall understanding of the roles and responsibilities in a Six Sigma project. In the typical Lean Six Sigma project, often the *Leaner* Practitioner will need to assume several roles. Understanding how each role should function independently offers insight as well as a solid checklist.

Activities involved in a Six Sigma project are outlined in the standard as gathering data, extracting information from that data, designing a solution and ensuring the desired results are obtained. ISO 13053-1 states that a reliable financial management model should be in place before beginning a process improvement.

In contrast, the ASQ-SSBOK, specifically notes that Six Sigma project awareness should include an understanding of market share, margin and revenue growth. Specific emphasis being placed on:

- Net Present Value (NPV)
- Return-on-Investment (ROI)
- Cost of Quality (COQ)

ISO 13053-1 promotes a basic maturity model. Maturity models are popular in other process improvement programs as well. Maturity model levels are intended to be used as markers and milestones. These levels may also be used to monitor success and to build evaluation metrics. These levels of maturity are summarized as:

- Level 1—the starting point
- Level 2—managed
- Level 3—defined
- Level 4—quantitatively managed
- Level 5—optimized

This model is familiar to students of Capability Maturity Model Integrated (CMMI). CMMI is a process improvement approach that is designed to improve enterprise-wide performance. CMMI is often used in defense contracts or software-related projects. According to the Software Engineering Institute (SEI), CMMI helps "integrate traditionally separate organizational functions, set process improvement goals and priorities, provide guidance for quality processes and provide a point of reference for appraising current processes."

Voice of the Customer (VOC) is emphasized in ISO 13053-1. The ASQ-SSBOK also includes references to VOC. VOC is defined as attention to customer feedback and understanding customer requirements. Customer requirements are also known as Critical-to-Quality (CTQ) factors. CTQ factors are more heavily stressed in Lean Six Sigma as compared to ISO 13053-1 or ASQ-SSBOK, thus exceeding the objectives of both documents. In LSS, Voice of the Employee (VOE) as well as the Voice of the Business (VOB) and Voice of the Process (VOP) are considered along with VOC.

As with all documents related to Six Sigma or Lean Six Sigma, ISO 13053-1 fully explains the Sigma statistic and normal distribution table by using the term Defects per Million Opportunities (DPMO).

ISO 13053-1 discusses Cost-of-Poor Quality (CoPQ) and relies on the Total Quality Management (TQM) definition of this term. CoPQ is incurred by producing and fixing defects resulting from an internal or external failure. Lean Six Sigma confirms this definition, but also includes what-if scenarios in the explanation of CoPQ. For example, how much would it cost not to do something? How much revenue would be lost?

The ISO 13053-1 standard explains roles within a Six Sigma project and their basic responsibilities to the project. For each role, a competency model is included as well as training suggestions, to achieve these designations. Roles outlined in this standard consist of:

- Champion
- Yellow Belt
- Green Belt
- Black Belt
- Master Black Belt
- Deployment Manager

These terms are universally accepted in Six Sigma, but Lean Six Sigma often includes the following roles and responsibilities:

- White Belt
- Process Owner
- Sponsor

The ASQ-SSBOK does not go into detail about the various roles and responsibilities, but does place a premium on things not included in the ISO 13053-1 document such as team types. The team types include:

- Formal
- Informal

- Virtual
- Cross-Functional
- Self-Directed

The ASQ-SSBOK includes sections on team facilitation, team dynamics, team communication, as well as time management of the team. This document also notes the various stages of a team that include:

1. Forming
2. Storming
3. Norming
4. Performing
5. Adjourning

Although information on teaming is not currently included in ISO 13053-1, the information provided by ASQ-SSBOK and team building principles used in Lean Six Sigma practices may be considered supporting documentation for the roles and responsibilities and competency models outlined in ISO 13053-1.

ISO 13053-1 outlines how to prioritize projects and offers suggestions for project selection originally introduced by Edwards Deming that includes considerations such as:

- Are there measures?
- Will the potential project improve customer satisfaction?
- Is the potential project aligned to at least one of the business measures?

Project Scoping, as well as process inputs and outputs, are discussed prior to introducing the DMAIC model. Project scoping and documentation of the scope are crucial activities for CI and OE initiatives as well. The *Leaner* Practitioner can often help in the CI and OE effort by clarifying the scope.

The ISO 13053-1 standard documents the five phases of the DMAIC model. The phases are covered more in-depth in Part Two of the book, *Lean Six Sigma Curriculum Development and Self-Study for the Global Professional.* ISO 13053-1 captures essential information for each phase of the DMAIC.

ISO 13053-2

The primary purpose of 13053-2 is to introduce tools that will help execute the DMAIC process. The following tools are introduced along with individual fact sheets:

- Affinity Diagram
- Brainstorming
- Cause and Effect Diagram
- Control Charts
- Critical-to-Quality Tree Diagram
- Data Collection Plan
- Descriptive Statistics
- Design of Experiment
- Determination of Sample
- FMEA (Failure Mode and Effects Analysis)
- Gantt Chart
- Hypothesis Testing
- Indicators of Key Performance
- Kano
- Measurement Systems
- Monitoring/Control Plan
- Normality Testing
- Prioritization Matrix
- Process Mapping and Process
- Project Charter
- Project Review
- QFD (Quality Function Deployment—House of Quality)
- RACI (Responsible, Accountable, Consulted and Informed) Matrix
- Regression and Correlation
- Reliability
- ROI (Return-on-Investment) Costs and Accountability
- Services Delivery
- SIPOC
- Value Stream
- Waste

ASQ-SSBOK and Lean Six Sigma Toolkit recognize the above reference tools. Students of OE or CI programs likewise use these tools. However, the ASQ-SSBOK does not offer specific instructions or fact sheets for these tools.

Lean Six Sigma philosophy will consider the scalability of the tool when making a tool decision. For example, if the project is small, tools such as Design of Experiment (DOE), Hypothesis Testing and QFD may not be useful. LSS theory also supports the thought that if the tool is not necessary, it may be abandoned. LSS further believes it is acceptable to modify a tool or use a tool creatively. These concepts are not promoted in ISO 13053-2 or the ASQ-SSBOK.

The ASQ-SSBOK also covers Design for Six Sigma (DFSS) which is not covered in ISO 13053-2. Although the standard does list and explain several tools that may be applied to DFSS projects. Lean Six Sigma addresses DFSS, but generally refers to it as Design for Lean Six Sigma (DFLSS).

DFSS or DFLSS is a process methodology used when no existing process is in place. A popular DFSS model is Define-Measure-Analyze-Design-Verify (DMADV). The first three phases of the model are the same as the DMAIC model which is why it is a popular choice for the *Leaner* Practitioner. The argument for DFSS is that some process improvements must be created from scratch and therefore require a design component.

ASQ-SSBOK places more emphasis on specific statistics and manual calculations. ISO 13053-2 promotes statistical thinking captured within the tools as opposed to individual statistical knowledge. Lean Six Sigma tends to slant toward the use of MS Excel-based statistical software with the intent of simplifying statistical concepts.

In summary, if the *Leaner* Practitioner has not worked in an ISO environment, reviewing ISO 9001:2008 is essential. This standard is valuable to the *Leaner* Practitioner even if certification is not the goal. ISO standards, in general, provide strong and defendable guidelines on what should be done to implement, monitor and evaluate process improvements. This standard provides specific instructions for a successful QMS.

The introduction of ISO 13053 for Six Sigma provides a visual roadmap for the *Leaner* Practitioner. It enhances the credibility of process improvement procedures and provides a common vocabulary and guidelines that may be implemented and understood worldwide. The *Leaner* Practitioner should also review and understand the ASQ-SSBOK as well as various Lean Six Sigma toolkits. The concepts governing CI and OE are equally important to consider.

The *Leaner* Practitioner should remember that all process improvements, best practices, standards, theories and methodologies interact with basic project management principles.

12

ISO 21500—Guide to Project Management

Process Improvement (PI) programs depend on project management skills to execute and sustain improvement activities. Project management is the discipline of planning, organizing, securing and managing resources to achieve specific goals. Today, the *Leaner* Practitioner must work to make these activities Lean and agile.

Internationally, project management relies heavily on policy and leadership models supported by the organization or culture. The *Leaner* Practitioner must also be aware of compliance issues governing the information technology (IT) activities of a specific country. Most enterprise-wide process improvements will include an IT component.

Lean Six Sigma has always considered basic project management essential to successful process improvement. There are many synergies between project management theory and Lean Six Sigma. Both basic project management and Lean Six Sigma are interested in establishing a sound plan, communicating with stakeholders and conducting regular reviews. Likewise, project management and Lean Six Sigma are concerned with managing the schedule and containing costs. *Leaner* Practitioners are encouraged to use templates from project management, especially those templates that focus on resource management and project execution.

Throughout the Define-Measure-Analyze-Improve-Control (DMAIC) model, used by Lean Six Sigma, project management tools are used. However, dedicated project management does not occur until the second half of the *Improve* phase. This is when a project plan is designed and executed.

Before building a project plan for process improvement, the Lean Six Sigma model strongly encourages defining the problem, creating a clear picture of the current condition and analyzing that condition. These activities are accomplished in the *Define, Measure* and *Analyze* phases. In the next, phase, *Improve,* the solutions are listed and a pilot is performed. If the pilot is successful, a project plan is designed and executed.

In other process improvement programs, a project plan is designed much earlier in the process. A premium is often placed on the project plan as proof work will be accomplished. The *Leaner* Practitioner needs to be aware of this expectation when working in various countries as well as when working with organizations who have established a formal Project Management Office (PMO).

Even in LSS, project management activities have room to be *Leaner* and more agile. For example, daily decision-making may not be delegated efficiently. Cross training opportunities may be overlooked. There may not be a strategy to educate the team on LSS tools designed to improve critical-thinking skills.

Lean thinking begins with identifying and reducing waste. Waste may be defined as anything that cannot be connected to customers' needs. A *Leaner* Practitioner should frame work, whenever possible, using the Work Break-down Structure (WBS) method. A WBS is an outline of all the tasks that need to be accomplished. Primary tasks are given whole numbers such as 1, 2 or 3. Subtasks are given designations such as 1.1, 2.1 or 3.1. Tasks related to the subtasks are recorded as 1.1.1 or 1.1.2. The theory is to break the task down to the smallest component in order to judge the time and effort required. This method is also a quick way to identify any unnecessary steps in the process.

Lean project management requires being familiar with core documents related to project management best practices. These materials continue to evolve. For example, the International Organization for Standardization (ISO) has created a new international standard for Project Management, referred to as *ISO 21500: Guide to Project Management.* This standard is designed to increase global awareness of project management. The primary purpose of the ISO 21500 is to enable multi-national organizations to coordinate their project management processes and systems. The *Leaner* Practitioner should benefit from this document since it strives to create a common universal language around project management concepts.

Other respected documents that outline the project management approach include the Project Management Body of Knowledge (PMBOK®) supported by the Project Management Institute (PMI) and PRojects IN

Controlled Environments 2 (PRINCE2®) endorsed by the UK government are also internationally accepted collaterals.

The *Leaner* Practitioner should stay aware, that at some point, a process improvement effort simply becomes a series of small projects that must be executed. This requires using project management theory as well as project management tools. Being familiar with the new ISO standard for project management as well as the PMBOK® and PRINCE2® serves the *Leaner* Practitioner well, as a solid educational platform. The following section explains these documents beginning with the PMBOK®.

PMBOK® management requires:

- Recognizing that projects are temporary—there is a beginning and an end
- Using a validated decision process to determine if a project should be done (risk assessment)
- Considering factors related to timing, cost, quality and resources
- Developing and articulating project scope
- Knowing how to successfully close out a project and document any successes

The PMBOK® has been recognized by the American National Standards Institute (ANSI) as an American National Standard (ANSI/PMI 99-001-2008) and by the Institute of Electrical and Electronics Engineers (IEEE) as the best guide for representing terminology and guidelines.

The PRINCE2® methodology encompasses the management, control and organization of a project. It involves a highly integrated approach to project management, which includes specific inputs and outputs. It is a process-based, structured project management methodology that high-lights how eight components, when understood and effectively addressed, can reduce risks in all types of projects.

In many cases, the *Leaner* Practitioner will be working for a company that has already adopted a formal project management process. Lean Six Sigma is an advocate of working within any formalized program to make that program better, faster and more cost effective.

The following information will provide an accelerated overview and highlights of *ISO Standard 12500: Guide to Project Management*, the PMBOK® and PRINCE2®. For the most part, there are more similarities than difference.

ISO 21500: Guide to Project Management states that for a project to be successful it should:

- Select appropriate processes to meet the project objectives
- Use a defined approach to develop or adapt the product specifications
- Comply with requirements to satisfy the project sponsor, customer and other stakeholders
- Define and manage the project scope within the constraints while considering the project risks and resource needs to produce the project deliverables
- Ensure proper support from each performing organization, including commitment from the customer and project sponsor

It is vital to note that content in ISO 21500, the PRINCE2® components and processes, as well as the knowledge areas in the PMBOK®, are consistent. The PMBOK® is the most detailed account of project management terms and processes, PRINCE2® concentrates more on applied knowledge and ISO 21500 provides a strong basic framework for a DMAIC project.

The PMBOK® supports nine knowledge areas. All process improvement programs recognize that basic project management must be in place before process improvement may begin.

- Integration Management
- Scope Management
- Time Management
- Cost Management
- Quality Management
- Human Resource Management
- Communications Management
- Risk Management
- Project Procurement Management

The PMBOK® also promotes that the following phases are necessary for a successful project:

- Initiating
- Planning
- Executing
- Monitoring and Controlling
- Closing

PRINCE2® processes highlight the following activities:

- Planning (continued throughout)
- Starting up a project
- Directing the project
- Initiating the project
- Managing stage boundaries
- Controlling a stage
- Managing product delivery
- Closing a project

Other business activities in PRINCE2® include:

- Defining the organization structure for the project management team
- Planning a Product/Service-based approach

Here is a simple comparison of the Main Topics in the PMBOK® Knowledge Area and PRINCE2® Components

PMBOK® Knowledge Area	PRINCE2® Components
Integration	Combined Processes and Components, Change Control
Scope, Time, Cost	Plans, Business Case
Quality	Quality, Configuration Management
Risk	Risk
Communications	Controls
Human Resources	Organization (limited)
Procurement	Not Covered

ISO 21500 is attempting to establish standards that can be adopted world-wide. PRINCE2® is a general framework, while PMI (Project Management Institute) focuses more on techniques. The big pluses of PRINCE2® are the following. Other recognized forms of project management accepted methodologies include, but are not limited to:

- Traditional Project Management Method
- Process-Based Project Management Methodology
- Agile for Project Management
- Critical Chain Project Management (CMPP)

Traditional Project Management is an approach that recognizes the same five developmental components as the PMBOK®. It does not place as much emphasis on the knowledge area and is less flexible.

Process-Based Project Management Methodology is an approach that uses maturity models. Examples would be Capability Maturity Model Integrated (CMMI®), a process improvement program developed by the Software Engineering Institute, a part of Carnegie Mellon University. Another example would be Software Process Improvement and Capability Estimation (SPICE also known as ISO/IEC15504).

Agile for Project Management is seen as a series of relatively small tasks. These tasks are flexible and executed on demand. Agile promotes being adaptive instead of being pre-planned. It also emphasizes human development initiatives. Agile techniques are best used in small-scale projects. This creates a strong alliance with Lean Six Sigma.

Critical Chain Project Management (CCPM) is a method of planning and managing projects that places the main emphasis on the resources required to execute project tasks. This method was developed by Eliyahu M. Goldratt. Goldratt was well-known for his work on Theory of Constraints (TOC) and his best-selling book from the 1990s, *The Goal.*

Process improvement projects will not work without a series of solid project management plans. As a reminder, in the DMAIC model, the project plan is not created until the *Improve* phase. *Define, Measure, Analyze* and much of the *Improve* activities are accomplished prior to building a project plan. This is intended to mistake-proof the process improvement. Nevertheless, each phase of the DMAIC process requires strong project management skills.

Understanding Project Management Life Cycle (PMLC) is valuable to the *Leaner* Practitioner some natural synergies exist. For example, the term "control" has a lot of the same dynamics as the DMAIC model. The *Leaner* Practitioner needs to pay attention to the DMAIC as well as PMLC.

Most project management methodologies/approaches agree that understanding the following areas are a key factor in successful project management:

- Integration Management
- Scope Management
- Time Management

- Cost Management
- Quality Management
- Human Resource Management
- Communications Management
- Risk Management
- Procurement Management

Projects are often defined as having a beginning and an end. However, in a Lean Six Sigma project, monitoring and controlling the process improvement is always on-going. A plan for sustainability is designed in the *Control* phase of the DMAIC model. Still, many of the activities a project manager generally uses to close out a project may be applied in the *Control* phase. For example, in the *Control* phase of the model, it is necessary to perform many project management activities such as documenting and/ or updating standard operating procedures, notifying stakeholders of the status and celebrating success.

Although many *Leaner* Practitioners use MS-Project to manage their process improvement projects, there are companies that offer specific Lean Six Sigma project management software. For new project managers and process improvement practitioners, these packages can be useful for templates and navigation.

Sometimes the methodology must be simplified to make the project *Leaner*. The Plan-Do-Check-Act (PDCA) is a popular alternative to the DMAIC. This methodology is also called the Deming Wheel.

- Plan: Identify an Opportunity and Plan for Change
- Do: Implement the Change on a Small Scale
- Check: Use Data to Analyze the Results of the Change and Determine Whether It Made a Difference
- Act: If the Change Was Successful, Implement It on a Wider Scale and Continuously Assess the Results. If the Change Did Not Work, Begin the Cycle Again

Lean Six Sigma, Total Quality Management and the PMBOK® endorse the PDCA model as a process improvement strategy. Although LSS prefers to use the DMAIC, the *Leaner* Practitioner recognizes that it is not always reasonable due to time constraints or the simplicity of the problem. A PDCA may be used within the various phases of the DMAIC. A PDCA may also be used prior to considering the DMAIC to determine the complexity of the problem.

Understanding basic project management materials will be beneficial to the *Leaner* Practitioner. However, it is important to note that there are some slight deviations from project management theory and process improvement. For example, a theory supported by the PMBOK® is that only two of the three process improvement conditions may exist at any one time. These three conditions are defined as improved: (1) quality, (2) speed and (3) expense.

In other words, if quality and speed are critical to the customer, it won't be inexpensive. If the most crucial factor to the customer is low expense and a fast turnaround, quality will suffer. This is a deviation from Lean Six Sigma thinking, although there are some process improvement programs that may side with the PMBOK® on this issue. LSS theory is that the right methodology can improve all three conditions. Therefore, the customer does not need to make this painful decision.

Another philosophy, where LSS and the PMBOK® differ, is the topic of scope creep. Scope represents the services that will be provided. Scope creep may be serious if a customer wants more service than was originally negotiated. Scope creep has the potential of distorting timelines and increasing cost. The PMBOK® is very concerned about scope creep and strongly cautions against the practice. Lean Six Sigma recognizes that scope creep could be a problem, but promotes always doing a little more than is expected. The purpose is to delight the customers with a few value-added activities.

When building a project plan, the *Leaner* Practitioner should stay cognizant and record any possible constraints. Constraints are conditions that may hinder project completion. For example, resource allocation might be a concern and therefore be listed as a constraint. Documenting constraints is the first step in building a risk-management strategy.

PMI CERTIFICATIONS

PMI offers several certifications. Each certification has different eligibility requirements:

- The CAPM® credential is designed for project team members and entry-level project managers, as well as qualified undergraduate and graduate students. The growing need for project management knowledge and proficiency bodes well for optimistic forecasts for IT practitioners

- PMP® (Project Management Practitioner)—One of the most widely recognized PM credentials requires the demonstration of a solid foundation of project management knowledge and practice
- PgMP™ (Program Management Practitioner)—This certification is geared toward those who manage multiple projects
- PMI-RMP (PMI Risk Management Practitioner)—This certification is designed for individuals who advise and make project decisions based upon risk factors
- PMI-SP (PMI Scheduling Practitioner)—Certification in project management scheduling

PRINCE2® CERTIFICATIONS

There are two PRINCE2® qualification levels: PRINCE2® Foundation and PRINCE2® Practitioner:

- PRINCE2® Foundation certification involves understanding the principles and terminology used in PRINCE2® and basic project management
- PRINCE2® Practitioner is the highest level of PRINCE2® qualification. This certification verifies that a practitioner understands how to apply PRINCE2® principles when running or managing a project

THE AMERICAN ACADEMY OF PROJECT MANAGERS

The American Academy of Project Managers has several degrees, each requiring a high level of experience. These are "awarded" certifications, based on a review of a person's experience and credentials:

- PME™ (Project Manager E-Business)
- CIPM™ (Certified International Project Manager)
- MPM™ (Master Project Manager)

There are other international organizations that offer project management certification. The Australian Institute of Project Management and the Project Management Association in Switzerland are two examples.

SELF-STUDY

For those interested in a self-study program related to international project management, topics to research would include:

- Project Management Tools and Techniques
- Microsoft Project Management Software
- Applied Project Management
- Cultural Awareness Training

Additional factors play a role in Lean Six Sigma and Project Management. The primary factors include:

- Change Management
- Leadership Development
- Measurement Systems Analysis
- Business Finance

In Lean Six Sigma and basic Project Management, the term Change Management refers primarily to the processes and documentation in place to ensure the change takes place or that the process is implemented. Change Management may also refer to the training necessary to prepare employees for the specific change.

> *Leadership Development* is defined as a program or activity that makes people become better leaders. An example of leadership development is a program for supervisors on how to more effectively communicate with their teams. Leadership is recognized as true component for success in a Lean Six Sigma organization. Lean Leadership expands to include understanding different cultures, generations and work ethics. Lean Leadership also is linked to:
> - An individual's ability to learn
> - Quality and nature of the leadership development program

- Genuine support for the leader's supervisor
- Choosing the right projects
- Choosing the right people
- Following the right methodology
- Clearly defining roles and responsibility

Measurement Systems Analysis (MSA) is a science that considers selecting the right measurement. It is necessary to study the measurement as well as the measurement device. Are measures reliable and valid? What is the measurement uncertainty? Calibration of equipment is an MSA issue.

Statistics is the science of making effective use of numerical data relating to groups of individuals or experiments. Six Sigma and Lean have always included the field of statistics when measuring and analyzing data. Now, a stronger weight is placed on choosing the right software and making sure that the statistic is valid.

Business Finance plays a stronger role for the *Leaner* Practitioner. Buy-in and continued support of a project cannot be based solely on statistical data. Choosing the appropriate Return-on-Investment formula and being able to measure project success, in financial terms, has become essential.

Moving forward as the *Leaner* Practitioner, it is imperative to remember that Lean Six Sigma is not just a matter of blending two highly successful process improvement methodologies, but rather encompassing a collection of bodies of knowledge.

In summary, stable project management plays a vital role in Lean Six Sigma. The *Leaner* Practitioner should stay aware, that at some point, a process improvement effort simply becomes a series of small projects that must be executed. This requires using project management theory as well as project management tools. Several project management approaches are available to the *Leaner* Practitioner.

The *Leaner* Practitioner should be familiar or certified in one of the main project management programs such as PMP® or PRINCE2®. Information contained in ISO 21500 should be reviewed. The *Leaner* Practitioner should look for ways to make basic project management activities *Leaner* by observing what steps can be eliminated without compromising the success of the process improvement.

Section IV

Leaner Environment

13

Leaner *Leadership*

A leader is one who knows the way, goes the way and shows the way.

John Maxwell

Leaner Leadership encompasses all the things mentioned in leadership basics. For example, similar to general leadership principles, the *Leaner* Leader's role in an organization is to provide direction and alignment with the organization. But the additional responsibilities of the *Leaner* Leader also include:

- Aligning purpose process people and the methodology to build a culture of continuous improvement
- Dealing with issues around creating change and improving business results
- Introducing the concept that a process improvement is not worthwhile without a sustainability component

Naturally, the *Leaner* Leader needs to be well-versed in problem-solving critical thinking. Generally speaking, this means an in-depth knowledge of the Plan-Do-Check-Act methodology (PDCA), discussed earlier in this book. The *Leaner* Leader should embrace a teachable scalable approach to business activities.

The *Leaner* Leader as well as the *Leaner* Practitioner should understand and be able to relate basic Lean practices. Summarized, they include:

- Identifying value
- Mapping the value stream for the purposes of identifying and reducing or eliminating waste

- Testing the flow to make sure the remaining steps run smoothly. Strong flow should have no interruptions, delays or bottlenecks
- Ensuring "Pull" is now being utilized as opposed to "Push." With improved flow time-to-market can be improved. This makes it easier to deliver products or services as are needed "just in time"
- Moving toward perfection

The *Leaner* Leader needs to have the ability to implement Lean practices in a transformational way that supports the organizational development alongside process improvement.

Typically, a Lean implementation involves an initial value stream mapping defining the journey of the process that is a candidate for improvement. This can use a method called Gemba involved Walk. The Gemba Walk involves walking the process for following the paperwork that leads to the successful delivery of the product or service.

In this Gemba Walk exercise, the *Leaner* Leader needs to be able to decide who are the most appropriate people to be invited on the walk. At a minimum, the team should include a subject matter expert and employees that work with the processes on a continual basis. In some cases, it can also include the vendor or supplier or member of the senior management team.

One of the biggest goals of *Leaner* Leadership is to ensure these goals are being met:

- Defining the service demand
- Understanding the lead time
- Matching up supply to the demand
- Eliminating or reducing waste in the process including lead time and cost

DEFINING THE SERVICE DEMAND

Defining the desire of consumers and internal customers Means Paying Attention to the Voice of the Customer (VOC) as well as the Voice of Employees. During this process it is important to understand the specific business needs and expectations of both the VOC and VOE.

The leadership role in defining the service demand requires facilitation and motivation skills prior to even considering execution.

Does the service or product meet the specific requirements of the VOC? Does the VOE understand these requirements and there is a process capability to meet these requirements successfully?

The nature of the demand is a much easier concept to understand:

- What is the demand?
- How much time is needed to meet demand?
- How frequently does the demand need to be met?
- Who is requesting the demand and why?
- Where and when is the initial starting point?
- How will we know the demand has been met?

HOW MUCH TIME IS NEEDED TO MEET THE DEMAND?

Basically, the formula is simply about understanding the actual demand and then forecasting time to meet that demand. Companies need to give themselves flexibility to consider their schedule as well as making sure they have the resources to meet that demand.

HOW FREQUENTLY DOES THE DEMAND NEED TO BE MET?

The *Leaner* Practitioner is simply trying to match the frequency of the demand to the demands of an ever-changing market. It is a reoccurring demand, the company needs to tenuously assess its ability to meet that demand, along with other emerging customer expectations.

WHO IS REQUESTING THE DEMAND AND WHY?

A strong understanding of who is requesting the demand and why is crucial to the success of *Leaner* leadership. It allows the leader to ensure they are working on the right set of solutions and guiding and motivating the team in the right direction. By understanding the root cause of the demand, the leader can gear all efforts toward that result.

WHERE AND WHEN IS THE INITIAL STARTING POINT?

Understanding location and timelines is crucial to leading people in the right direction. It also eliminates any misunderstandings.

HOW WILL WE KNOW THE DEMAND HAS BEEN MET?

It is important to understand everyone's concept of success prior to leading a project.

Educating the workforce on how to engage in process improvement has extreme merit. Lean Six Sigma recognizes the analytical business processes that must take place, but balances that approach with the recognition that people are the drivers. Other process methodologies would agree, however, Lean Six Sigma emphasizes the role of the leader along with understanding change management and team dynamics.

The leadership styles, used in business, began getting attention in the early 1900s. Over the decades, these styles have been repackaged and renamed. The four styles originally given the most respect, due to research performed, included:

- Bureaucratic
- Charismatic
- Democratic
- Reactive

According to the most popular research, bureaucratic leaders are structured and follow established procedures. Charismatic leaders lead by inspiration. Democratic leaders are concerned with consensus. Reactive leaders make decisions immediately without considering feedback from other employees.

In 1939, a group of researchers led by psychologist Kurt Lewin identified only three main types of leadership styles. This work was based on studying groups of children and is still highly respected today. The children were assigned to one of the following groups:

- Authoritarian
- Participative
- Laissez-Faire

The autocratic leader provides clear expectations and there is an obvious division between leader and follower. The participative or democratic leader offers guidance to group members, but this type of leader also participates in the group, allowing input from other group members. The laissez-faire leader delegated most tasks to the members of the team.

Lewan's research indicated that team members were the most productive in autocratic environments, but more creative in participative environments. His research also stated that the least productive and creative environments were the groups designated as laissez-faire.

Lewan's research deemed the democratic leadership style as the most effective. He believed that although autocratic leadership appeared to offer the most productivity, it was the leadership style most likely to be abused. However, Lewin also believed that autocratic leadership was effective when their deadlines did not allow for group decision-making and/or when the leader demonstrated that they were the most knowledgeable member of the team.

Originally, all research performed on leadership styles promoted the idea that everyone had a specific style. Much merit was given to the idea that it was necessary for a good leader to identify their core style in order to be enlightened and to expand their leadership abilities. Newer thinking is based on situational leadership. This means that the leadership style would be dependent on the actual situation.

Leadership styles have been expanded to include the following:

- Relation-Oriented Leader
- Servant Leader
- Transformational Leader
- Task-Oriented Leader

Relation-Oriented Leaders are also referred to as people-oriented leaders. In this style, the leader tries to support and mentor the team members as opposed to setting the supreme direction.

Servant Leaders has become a popular theory. This leader does not officially act as leader, but takes a more informal approach and makes decisions collectively by consulting with the team. It is like democratic leadership. However, most literature indicates that this type of leadership is more sensitive than the democratic leader, as this leader is concerned about how people feel and why they voted the way they did as opposed to simply making consensus-based decisions.

Transformational Leaders provide motivation to the team, giving them a reason to adopt a change. It is like charismatic leadership, but the focus isn't on the leader's personal traits or popularity.

Task-Oriented Leaders are known for focusing on what the team needs to achieve. This leader is like result-oriented leaders, but is more aware of the needs and welfare of the team members.

Most current leadership research suggests that all leaders need to be more engaged if they hope to lead teams in the right direction. Leaders need to act as a catalyst for change.

The article, "Leaders Asleep at the Wheel," states that it is no mystery why so many leaders are asleep at the wheel and not as fully engaged in the leadership process.

These days it is not uncommon for the best and the brightest to opt for opportunities that offer more life balance. Ten years ago, a bevy of baby boomers emerged, excited about the prospects of entering senior leadership roles. A decade later, the bloom is off the rose. The entire do-more-with-less philosophy is partially to blame. Equally to blame, however, is the fact that culture changed. Now leaders are expected to listen, be open and seek differing opinions.

Smart individuals, who want to lead, get with the program and understand the new culture. Unfortunately, there are still some who have not learned these new principles. Consequently, there are not enough qualified people to handle all the leadership roles available. The void is often filled by people with no innate ability to lead and/or by those with no formal leadership training.

These leaders are asleep at the wheel. They are sometimes difficult to identify because they are almost always incredibly busy. Being asleep at the wheel doesn't mean that they are lethargic or lazy. Their hectic schedule often causes them to miss the big picture. It becomes about finishing projects as opposed to finishing projects right. The process becomes unimportant.

Leaders who are asleep at the wheel are certain that they are smarter than the rest of us. They know what we need and want, without asking. They talk a lot about listening, but rarely do. This occurs frequently, even in some of the more minor leadership roles. These leaders suffer from a serious lack of vision. They honestly believe that they are in touch with the very pulse of their community. Because they are so certain they are right about everything they miss the obvious. They may represent their position as the voice of an organization or that of an entire industry.

Leaders who are asleep at the wheel aren't totally to blame. The life balance scenario is very appealing. Plenty of people want to work or serve their organization. They just don't want to be in charge. This means many leadership decisions go unchallenged. Unfortunately, this makes the leader feel more powerful and even the slightest criticism can be interpreted by the leader as a major threat. This results in people realizing that speaking up may have consequences.

The financial fiascos that come to light on a regular basis are perfect examples of leaders asleep at the wheel. Although it will be a point of debate for many years to come as to who was responsible for the debacle, there were many leaders of departments simply not paying attention. They had been encouraged not to worry, by their supervisors. They were receiving compensation at a level that must surely mean they were doing the right thing. No one questioned the situation and those who did were deemed ungrateful or unworthy.

Leaders who are asleep at the wheel rush to judgment, misuse their resources and repeatedly use failure-prone tactics to make decisions. They are incapable of changing things on their own or seeing the situation through a different lens. As good members of a team, everyone needs to be prepared to speak up, ask questions and hold our leaders accountable.

Leaner Leaders seek "mission-critical projects," and they provide the management energy and horsepower to free up resources. But more than that, Lean Six Sigma Leaders have the vision to "imagine the future." An effective Lean Six Sigma leader identifies high potential employees and understands the value of training.

Leadership is an essential quality which all project managers are presumed to possess. But the amount of actual ability is a variable. Some come by it naturally as a result of inherited qualities. Others may benefit from formal leadership development. Leadership development refers to any activity that enhances the quality of leadership.

A critical skill for leaders is the ability to manage their own learning. The first step is to conduct a self-assessment. Leadership development is a continuous process and not an annual event Adapting leadership styles to each person's needs and not being afraid to collect input from others is crucial.

The personal attributes and character of leaders are varied. The competencies (knowledge, skills and abilities) that a person needs in order to lead at a time in an organization depend on a variety of factors. However, most people will agree that a good leader should possess common sense and judgment.

How an organization is structured often dictates the leadership role in a Lean Six Sigma project. For example, organizations that favor matrix management can be both a positive and negative force for the Lean Six Sigma leader. In this type of company, a link between senior management functions and self-contained work cells is sometimes maintained through a matrix structure in which personnel assigned to functions are deployed temporarily to the cells. This approach maintains some of the advantages of specialization while facilitating coordination within cells.

This arrangement is not easy to run. The managers of the various work cells may compete with their counterparts for the services, such as quality control and maintenance. Managers of functions may be concerned that temporary assignments of their personnel to cells may become permanent. No consensus on the ideal solution has emerged, although some continuity of staffing may be needed for the success of the project, permanent assignments may impair the ability of the functions to maintain specialized knowledge.

As noted earlier, the new *Leaner* tools focus on continuous improvement as a guiding principle. The road to quality is paved with small incremental improvements. Major sweeping changes seldom work. As this country moves its business style from control to management to leadership, we are finding that the people doing the work are the most capable of identifying changes necessary to improve quality. Leadership must listen and implement changes rather than direct.

Leaner Leaders are encouraged to think in a new way and may be involved in any of the following activities:

- Acting as a catalyst
- Asking the right questions
- Creating a responsive project solution
- Developing options and alternatives
- Discovering and exposing ideas
- Effecting timely decision making
- Establishing effective and efficient project start-up
- Establishing team ownership
- Expediting decision making
- Facilitating the design team
- Identifying and clarifying organizational structure
- Improving communication
- Integrating customers into the total team

- Orienting the total team to a mutual goal
- Providing a framework by which to benchmark project success
- Reaching design consensus
- Synthesizing ideas
- Testing options and alternatives
- Uncovering opportunities
- Understanding total requirements

In Western models of corporate organization, there are leadership issues that need to align with vertical integration, horizontal diversification, growth by merger, acquisition and shareholder interests. Lean Six Sigma encourages working in tandem rather than against the business system.

Successful *Leaner* Leadership efforts are generally linked to:

- Individual learner characteristics
- The quality and nature of the leadership development program
- Genuine support from the leader's supervisor

The way that leadership development differs in Lean Six Sigma is that typical leadership programs focus on the development of the leader, such as the personal attributes desired in a leader, desired ways of behaving, ways of thinking or feeling. *Leaner* Leadership focuses more on the development of leadership as a process. This includes the social influence process, interpersonal relationships and team dynamics. The advantage of this approach is that a person, who may not feel that they are a natural leader, may be more comfortable learning a process than changing their overall personality. *Leaner* Leadership is also very flexible and supports changing strategy when necessary.

Leaders play a critical role during change implementation. Effective *Leaner* leadership will reduce the adverse reaction to change.

In companies where a Project Management Office is present, the *Leaner* Leader must understand the dynamics since all projects will be monitored through this entity.

Typically, the accepted functions of a PMO are:

- To provide support and guidance to managers in project implementation
- To introduce the right process and evolve suitable methodology aimed at developing acceptable standards

- Design training programs to prepare the team members to efficiently perform their assigned tasks
- Continuous monitoring of project progress and mentoring the team members
- Select, introduce and oversee use of appropriate software tools
- Constitute a panel of program managers and train them to run inter-related multiple projects
- Timely resource allocation to complete work within specified time limits

Choosing the right person to implement and lead the *Leaner* movement in the workplace involves choosing a leader who understands the importance the scalability for the product or service and the need to keep all parties involved motivated. This person should have the ability not only to implement change, but to inspire change as well. Leadership that works is committed to continuous improvement. Commitment to continuous improvement requires the ability to manage change which is the topic of the next chapter.

14

Change Management

The greatest danger in times of turbulence is not the turbulence – it is to act with yesterday's logic.

Peter Drucker

It is often the job of the *Leaner* Leader or the *Leaner* Practitioner to champion the change management effort. In some companies, this effort is assigned to the Process Improvement Department. In other companies, the responsibilities are assigned to the Human Resources Department. To confuse matters even more, sometimes department managers are randomly assigned this duty without any training or knowledge of expectations.

In this chapter, the term Change Manager (CM), is used as an umbrella term to encompass all professionals who have been assigned to the change management function. Very often, the CM is synonymous with the *Leaner* Leader or the *Leaner* Practitioner. Since all Lean Practitioners assume some sort of leadership and change management role, this chapter uses the term *Leaner* Practitioner to include a *Leaner* Leader as well.

Change related to Lean Six Sigma must be compelling. In a *Leaner* organization, integrating the openness to change into the daily work life is essential. No one wants to be in a situation where change is a result of crisis. As demand changes, so does the supply. As resource capability changes, there needs to be a constant evaluation of how this change can be reconfigured. When talking about resource capability, to support the change, it is not only about Human Resources. Non-Human Resources need to also be considered as part of the change model. This would include technology tools and equipment.

Change management is a structured approach to transitioning organizations, individuals and teams from a current state to a desired future state. However, when the term "change management" became popular in the business community everyone was a little confused.

For example, in the information technology industry, change management related to standardizing business processes. In systems engineering, the term change management is used to explain the change management procedure. This would include how the change is requested through how the change is implemented. In Human Resources, change management has to do with people issues and how they will react to the change. Lean Six Sigma generally refers to CM as anything related to change, including all the different perspectives related to change management.

A common factor with nearly all change management initiatives is resistance. Generally, people are resistant to change out of a fear of losing something at a personal level. The *Leaner* Practitioner may need to assure employees that Lean Six Sigma is a tool, not a replacement, for processes the employee currently controls.

It is also wise to introduce change in phases to give everyone the opportunity to adapt. One advantage to using the DMAIC methodology is that the model clearly states ideas need to be piloted prior to rollout. This helps with the resistance factor. Successful pilots demonstrate the probability of success and reduce the fear factor.

The *Measure* Phase of the DMAIC is also crucial in the change management effort. Helping employees understand the current state of a process lessens speculation. When the *Leaner* Practitioner takes reliable and valid measurements in the beginning and shares the current state with the employees, when the change is realized, project managers can introduce a simple comparison chart. This is where we were. This is where we are today. Buy-in is not an issue because the process improvement is apparent. When the project manager does not take time to validate the current state, employees are often confused as to why the change is necessary.

Change management anxiety can also be contributed to participants believing they do not have enough time to implement the change. Lean Six Sigma, again, positions itself as a program that will help increase time and focus resources. Lean Six Sigma has several simple tools that can be implemented immediately to make things work faster.

There is a strong argument that true change agents should be reporting into the executive level of leadership. However, in some companies, the topic of change management is handled through the Human

Resources Department. Although this is not an ideal situation, if the company is invested in this idea, it would help the project manager to align with change leaders in the Human Resources Department. Therefore, the topic of change management is often covered in Human Resource Management programs.

Change management professionals who have a background or education in basic project management have a clear advantage. Being well versed in an improvement methodology, such as Lean Six Sigma, is even a bigger plus. *Leaner* Practitioners who can present a business case with an undeniable Return-on-Investment will be respected. Having a true handle on cost/time estimates, analytical thinking process and fact-based strategies will open doors.

Understanding and using statistics to convey thoughts raise the bar on necessary conversations such as:

- Legal compliance related to change management
- Developing a recruiting and retention strategy
- Performance management
- Job design
- Knowledge management
- Human resource information systems
- Strategic, operational and administrative issues

The role of the *Leaner* Practitioner is typically divided into three main categories—strategic, operational and administrative. In today's world, *Leaner* Practitioners are expected to act with confidence in all three categories. Lean Six Sigma methodologies provide a framework for confidently capturing and presenting information in all three areas.

There are many other ways *Leaner* Practitioners may benefit from using Lean Six Sigma concepts. First, Leading Six Sigma methodology provides a solid path to implementing new projects. Second, learning to use the statistical information promoted in Six Sigma allows the *Leaner* Practitioner to make better, more informed decisions. Third, studying Six Sigma principles provides for better communication with project managers, technical staff and executive management.

Leaner Practitioners who also are responsible for health and safety issues will see a benefit to applying Six Sigma methodology to high risk environments. Six Sigma forces the practitioner to study the existing system. This may lead to identifying potential dangers. Whereas many safety programs focus only on satisfying lengthy compliance agendas, they do not position employees to think about future impact or identify future risk issues.

One area in which the *Leaner* Practitioner can be a strong contributor is designing metrics. It is necessary to distinguish which metrics are truly adding value to the organization. Measuring for measurement's sake is time consuming and contributes to waste. To determine which metric should be used, it is imperative to understand both the strategic initiatives of the department as well as the organization. Being familiar with the strategic initiatives is key to many HR processes such as performance reviews, job descriptions and employee orientation. Lean Six Sigma models all depend on proper measurement system and the *Leaner* Practitioner may have already compiled useful data that can be used in these metrics.

Internal benchmarking is an area that many *Leaner* Practitioners understand. Internal benchmarking involves the process of comparing a specific operation within the organization to another operation. Although the two operations do not need to be exact, they need to be similar. This process knowledge is very useful to the Six Sigma project team. Identifying Critical-to-Quality factors (CTQs) is not vastly different than identifying items that are critical to employee satisfaction. Another popular Lean Six Sigma model, SIPOC, Supplier, Inputs, Process, Output and Customer (SIPOC), discussed earlier in this book, is not a great stretch for the *Leaner* Practitioners. In the recruiting process, these areas must be identified to implement a successful program.

Leaner Practitioners also are astute at documenting best practices. This is another area where understanding the process is as important as understanding the subject matter. It is not unusual even in a structured Lean Six Sigma project for internal best practices to remain unidentified. This is usually because methods for communicating best practices do not exist. To be successful, organizations must implement a process that promotes and rewards the sharing of ideas.

Scorecards may be an area that the *Leaner* Practitioner has experience designing. Scorecards are an accepted way to keep track of business success. A successful business scorecard would promote a balance between long and short-term goals, financial and non-financial measures, as well as between internal and external perspectives. Implementation of a scorecard system requires translating the vision into operational or financial goals. Although the *Leaner* Practitioner may not have experience enterprise wide, most are skilled at doing this type of measurement for their own departments.

This experience benefits projects that use a scorecard system because there must be a commitment to a vision, a process and a communication plan to share with employees. The same competencies that allow a project manager to improve the quality and bottom line results may backfire without the necessary people skills.

At first, it may be difficult for a *Leaner* Practitioner to get the training necessary to be successful. There may not be the budget or a desire to formally educate administrative support staff.

Other areas that are a natural fit for a *Leaner* Practitioner trying to gain Lean Six Sigma experience include developing Lean Six Sigma retention strategies and creating job descriptions. Developing a rewards and recognition program, although promoted in Lean Six Sigma, rarely has a serious process owner. *Leaner* Practitioners need to seek out opportunities to become involved. A proactive approach will be noticed and appreciated. Although Lean Six Sigma does require formal education and training, any hands-on experience will make the concepts easier to digest.

Introducing Lean Six Sigma into an organization is a major change that will have a profound effect on a broad group of stakeholders. Managers and employees at many levels of the organization will be asked to engage in new behaviors. Those leading other initiatives may see Lean Six Sigma as a source of competition for resources, executive attention and organizational power. There may be confusion over how Lean Six Sigma fits within the large number of ongoing organizational programs such as Capability Maturity Model Integrated (CMMI) or ISO. Improvement does not happen without a plan.

Most executives will state that people are their most important resource. It makes sense that quality initiatives and continuous improvement programs should be adopted and applied by the change management group. The *Leaner* Practitioner can help determine which functions to measure and which metrics to be used. This can provide education on applying realistic benchmarking and in compiling a workable scorecard. The *Leaner* Practitioner can help reduce uncertainty and anxiety surrounding Lean Six Sigma and be a valuable resource to the Lean Six Sigma team.

Leaner Practitioners who are interested in studying and utilizing Six Sigma methodology are an asset to any company. They can improve processes in their own department, serve as a role model and assist in larger company projects.

Section V

Leaner Six Sigma Body of Knowledge and Competency Models

15

Leaner *Six Sigma Body of Knowledge Outline: Summarized Version (SSD Global Solution Version 6.1)*

The first entities attributed with blending Lean and Six Sigma were AlliedSignal and Maytag, independently in 1999. At that time, it was referred to as "Lean and Six," as both AlliedSignal and Maytag realized that the two methodologies complement one another. It was not until several years later that the term Lean Six Sigma became popular and only since 2004 that being certified as the Leader Practitioner gained recognition as a solid industry certification.

Over the past decade, Lean Six Sigma adopted many tools and ideologies that were not originally based in Lean or Six Sigma. The newer, *Leaner* Lean Six Sigma has been improved to capitalize on any tools or thoughts that contribute to process improvement. In other words, Lean Six Sigma has become better, faster and more cost effective as a methodology. In its new form, it is the only methodology that works in tandem with other process improvement methodologies.

Although Six Sigma is the dominant methodology in Lean Six Sigma, which is heavily influenced by Lean Thinking, the new more powerful Lean Six Sigma is comprised of several bodies of knowledge.

This document is an outline of the Lean Six Sigma Body of Knowledge (SSD Global Version 3.3). This body of knowledge is presented in four parts:

- Major Process Improvement Programs That Contributed to Lean Six Sigma (Section 1)
- Lean Six Sigma Knowledge (Section 2)
- Core Tools Used in Lean Six Sigma (Section 3)
- Implementation (Section 4)

1. **MAJOR PROCESS IMPROVEMENT PROGRAMS THAT CONTRIBUTED TO LEAN SIX SIGMA**
   1.1. **Primary Recognized Process Improvement Programs**
      1.1.1. Total Quality Management (TQM)
      1.1.2. International Standards Organization (ISO)
      1.1.3. Capability Maturity Model Integrated (CMMI)
      1.1.4. Six Sigma
         1.1.4.1. Defect Reduction
         1.1.4.2. DMAIC Model
         1.1.4.3. DFSS Model
         1.1.4.4. Statistical Thinking
         1.1.4.5. Recognizing Individual Tasks within a Process and Assigning Major Causes of Variation
            1.1.4.5.1. Common Cause Variability
            1.1.4.5.2. Special Cause Variability
         1.1.4.6. Stabilize Processes
      1.1.5. Lean Manufacturing
         1.1.5.1. Waste Reduction/Elimination
         1.1.5.2. Speed
         1.1.5.3. Voice of the Customer/Employee/Business/Process
      1.1.6. Additional Methodologies and Bodies of Knowledge That Play a Role in Lean Six Sigma
         1.1.6.1. Total Quality Management (TQM)
         1.1.6.2. Quality Body of Knowledge (Q-BOK™)
         1.1.6.3. Business Analysis Body of Knowledge (BABOK®)
         1.1.6.4. Project Management Body of Knowledge (PMBOK®)

1.1.6.5. Business Process Reengineering (BPR)
1.1.6.6. Change Management
1.1.6.7. Leadership Development
1.1.6.8. Measurement Systems Analysis
1.1.6.9. Statistics
1.1.6.10. Business Finance
1.1.6.11. Organizational Development

2. **LEAN SIX SIGMA**
   2.1. Systematic Approach to Reducing Waste and Eliminating Defects
       2.1.1. Statistical Thinking Blended with Voice of the Customer
       2.1.2. Better, Faster, More Cost-Effective Methods and Tools
       2.1.3. Uses DMAIC and DFSS Models
       2.1.4. Incorporates PDCA Model
   2.2. **Important Names in Lean Six Sigma**
       2.2.1. Shewhart
       2.2.2. Deming
       2.2.3. Juran
       2.2.4. Baldrige
       2.2.5. Taguchi
       2.2.6. Goldratt
       2.2.7. Ishikawa
   2.3. **Basic Quality Concepts**
       2.3.1. Customer Satisfaction

3.3.4.1.   3 Ps

    3.3.4.1.1.   People
    3.3.4.1.2.   Product
    3.3.4.1.3.   Process

3.3.4.2.   6 Ms

    3.3.4.2.1.   Machines
    3.3.4.2.2.   Methods
    3.3.4.2.3.   Materials
    3.3.4.2.4.   Measure
    3.3.4.2.5.   Mother Nature
    3.3.4.2.6.   Manpower

3.3.4.3.   6 Ws

    3.3.4.3.1.   What
    3.3.4.3.2.   Where
    3.3.4.3.3.   Why
    3.3.4.3.4.   Who
    3.3.4.3.5.   When
    3.3.4.3.6.   Which

3.3.4.4.   8 Ds—Short for the Eight Disciplines

    3.3.4.4.1.   Establish the Team
    3.3.4.4.2.   Describe the Problem
    3.3.4.4.3.   Develop an Interim Containment Plan
    3.3.4.4.4.   Determine Root Cause

16

Leaner *Six Sigma Body of Knowledge Outline: Full Narrative Version (SSD Global Solution Version 6.1)*

This document expands the concepts as outlined in the Lean Six Sigma Body of Knowledge (SSD Global Version 6.1) summary outline. The following information uses the Work Breakdown Structure (WBS) format.

The first entities attributed with blending Lean and Six Sigma were AlliedSignal and Maytag, independently in 1999. At that time, it was referred to as "Lean and Six" as both AlliedSignal and Maytag realized that the two methodologies complement one another. It was not until several years later that the term Lean Six Sigma became popular and only since 2004 that being certified as a Lean Six Sigma Green Belt or a Lean Six Sigma Black Belt has been recognized in the business community.

Over the past decade, Lean Six Sigma adopted many tools and ideologies that were not originally based in Lean or Six Sigma. The newer, *Leaner*, Lean Six Sigma has been improved to capitalize on any tools or thoughts that contribute to process improvement. In other words, Lean Six Sigma has become better, faster and more cost effective as a methodology. In its new form, it is the only methodology that works in tandem with other process improvement methodologies.

Although Six Sigma is the dominant methodology in Lean Six Sigma, which is heavily influenced by Lean Thinking, the new more powerful Lean Six Sigma is comprised of several bodies of knowledge.

This body of knowledge is presented in four sections:

- Major Process Improvement Programs That Contributed to Lean Six Sigma (Section 1)

- Lean Six Sigma (Section 2)
- Core Tools and Knowledge Used in Lean Six Sigma (Section 3)
- Implementation (Section 4)

MAJOR PROCESS IMPROVEMENT PROGRAMS THAT CONTRIBUTED TO LEAN SIX SIGMA

The Primary Recognized Process Improvement Programs

Total Quality Management

Total Quality Management (TQM) is the foundation of most process improvement programs. The core TQM strategy is to embed the awareness of quality throughout the entire organization. Both Six Sigma and Lean Manufacturing/Thinking promote concepts and tools first introduced by TQM. TQM also means continuously improving processes and products as well as reducing waste. Therefore, TQM aligns closely with Lean Six Sigma.

The major difference between Lean Six Sigma and TQM is that the tools used in Lean Six Sigma are updated and less labor intensive. Generally, the mission, goals and philosophy of TQM are also represented in Lean Six Sigma.

Many TQM ideas and problem-solving tools can be traced back to early 1920s, when statistical theory was applied to product quality control. The concept of applying mathematical and statistical models to improve product quality was further developed in Japan in the 1940s. This effort was led by U.S. Americans, such as Edwards Deming and Joseph Juran. Deming was responsible for popularizing the idea, whereas Juran wrote much of the original literature.

Deming was a protégé of Dr. Walter Shewhart. Juran also studied with Shewhart. Shewhart is sometimes referred to as the "father of statistical quality control." Shewhart's contribution to quality focuses on control charts, special/common cause variation and analytical statistical studies. Shewhart's work also concentrates on Statistical Process Control (SPC). Often SPC is studied as a sub-set of TQM. SPC studies various charts and graphs to determine and monitor process capability.

Beginning in the 1980s, a new phase of quality control and management began. The focus widened from quality of products to quality of all issues including service opportunities within an organization. It was determined that many of the same mathematical and statistical models used to identify, monitor and evaluate the quality of products could also be applied in the service industry.

In 1988, a significant step in quality management was made when the Malcolm Baldrige Award was established by the President of the United States. This national award recognizes companies for their quality contributions. Malcolm Baldrige was responsible for bringing quality to the government during the Reagan Administration. The Baldrige Program's mission is to improve the competitiveness and performance related to quality.

The Baldrige program was a direct result of the TQM movement and includes:

- Raising the awareness of performance excellence
- Providing organizational assessment tools and criteria
- Educating business leaders
- Recognizing national role models in quality

TQM is a set of management practices throughout an organization, geared to ensure that the organization consistently meets or exceeds customer requirements. In a TQM effort, all members of an organization participate in improving processes, products and services. Quality initiatives are not limited to the Quality Department.

Modern definitions of TQM include phrases such as: customer focus, the involvement of all employees, continuous improvement and the integration of quality management into the total organization.

Basic TQM supports:

- Line management ownership
- Employee involvement and empowerment
- Challenging quantified goals and benchmarking
- Focus on processes and improvement plans
- Specific incorporation in strategic planning
- Recognition and celebration

TQM has adopted several documents that are also used in other process improvement efforts to include the Lean Six Sigma program. Typically, these documents are identified by the following titles:

- Deming's 14 Points
- Deming's 7 Deadly Diseases
- The Deming Cycle
- Joseph Juran's Roadmap for Quality Leadership
- The Triple Constraint Model

In general terms, TQM is a management approach to long-term success through customer satisfaction and is based on the participation of all members of an organization in improving processes, products and services.

International Standards Organization

International Standards Organization (ISO), founded in 1947, is an international-standard-setting body composed of representatives from various national standards organizations (ISO). ISO has developed over 18,000 International Standards making it the largest standards-developing organization in the world. The ISO 9000 and ISO 14000 series are the most well-known. However, up to 1,100 new ISO standards are published every year.

The ISO 9000 family specifically addresses "Quality Management." This means what the organization does to fulfill:

- The customer's quality requirements and
- Applicable regulatory requirements, while aiming to
- Enhance customer satisfaction and
- Achieve continual improvement of its performance in pursuit of these objectives

The ISO 14000 family addresses "Environmental Management." This means what the organization does to:

- Minimize harmful effects on the environment caused by its activities and to
- Achieve continual improvement of its environmental performance

To be certified in an ISO standard, these steps are necessary:

- Locating and Selecting a Registrar—this is a company who is certified by ISO to make the initial assessment and provide suggestions for the *Leaner* Practitioner ISO program
- Creating an application and conducting a document review
- Participating in an assessment
- Completing the ISO registration
- Participating in a recertification effort

ISO Recertification efforts include gathering the proper measurements and articulating these measurements as well as identifying future opportunities for process improvement. There is also a time factor involved. Therefore, Lean Six Sigma often plays a primary role in ISO recertification.

Capability Maturity Model Integrated

Capability Maturity Model Integrated (CMMI) is another popular process improvement program. This integrated approach is intended to help an organization improve performance by recognizing certain levels of performance. CMMI can be used to guide process improvement across a project, a division or an entire organization.

In CMMI models with a staged representation, there are five maturity levels designated by the numbers 1 through 5:

1. Initial
2. Managed
3. Defined
4. Quantitatively Managed
5. Optimizing

CMMI was developed by the CMMI project, which was designed to improve the usability of maturity models by integrating many different models into one framework. The project consisted of members of industry, government and the Carnegie Mellon Software Engineering Institute (SEI). The main sponsors included the Office of the Secretary of Defense (OSD) and the National Defense Industrial Association.

Each level in the CMMI process requires detailed information gathering and analysis. The significance of Lean Six Sigma in CMMI is that often to move up one level, Lean Six Sigma practices need to be engaged.

Six Sigma

Defect Reduction

The Six Sigma problem-solving methodology is the most effective tool to quickly reduce and eliminate defects. It is a team-based methodology which works by systematically identifying and controlling the process variables that contribute to producing the defect or mistake.

DMAIC Model

Improvement of existing products or processes using the Six Sigma methodology is done in five steps:

- Define
- Measure
- Analyze
- Improve
- Control

Define

The purpose of the *Define* phase is to make sure that everyone understands the project and the goals of the process improvement effort. The basic steps include:

- Create a process improvement charter and process map
- Identify or define the problems in the *Leaner* Practitioner process that must be solved in order to meet or exceed the customer's specifications or expectations
- Identify and quantify customer requirements
- Identify and quantify the process output and defects that fall short of these requirements and create a problem statement
- State the project goal, which also must be a clear and measurable goal and include a time limit for the project's completion
- Determine the few vital factors that are Critical-to-Quality, which need to be measured, analyzed, improved and controlled

Measure

The purpose of the *Measure* phase is to get a strong as-is snapshot of how the process is currently behaving. The basic steps include:

- Select the Critical-to-Quality characteristics in your process. These are the outputs of the given process that are important to the customer. How is the process doing now?
- Define what that process output should be, which is done by looking at the customer requirements and the project goal
- Define the defect for the process. Remember, a defect is an output that falls outside the limits of customer's requirements or expectations and must be measurable
- Find the inputs to the process that contribute to defects
- Define the exact dollar impact of eliminating the defects in terms of increased profitability and/or cost savings
- Measure the defects that affect the Critical-to-Quality characteristics as well as any related factors
- Incorporate Measurement Systems Analysis—a method to make sure the defects are being measured properly

Analyze

The purpose of the *Analyze* phase is to review the measurements and information from the previous phase and determine, based on that information, what 3–5 solutions might be appropriate to solve the problem or roll out the activity.

- Determine root cause
- Identify variations that could be reduced
- Determine if correlation exists
- Do what-if scenarios
- Determine the timeline and cost of solutions
- Determine the sustainability of the solution

Improve

The purpose of the Improve phase is to choose a solution, implement the solution and be able to definitively prove that a process improvement has been accomplished. This is done by comparing the as-is state (the *Measure* phase) with conditions after the process improvement has been rolled out. Basic steps include:

- Articulate the 3–5 possible solutions
- Gain consensus on the best solution
- Pilot
- Create an execution plan (Project Plan) if the solution is successful in the pilot
- Choose another one of the 3–5 solutions if the pilot is not successful
- Rollout

Control

The purpose of the *Control* phase is to sustain the improvement. Basic steps include:

- Clearly articulating the process improvement achieved
- Creating a Control Plan to keep the process in place
- Designing a transition plan for the new owner

Design-for-Six-Sigma Model

Design-for-Six-Sigma, also known as Design-for-Lean-Six Sigma (DFSS or DFLSS) is applicable only in situations where a new product or service needs to be designed or re-designed from the very beginning. Many supporters of the DMAIC design believe that this is accomplished in the *Analyze* and *Improve* phases of the DMAIC model. However, supporters of DFSS believe a design component is necessary. Recently, models based on the DMAIC thinking process that do not have a design component are also referred to as DFSS or DFLSS models.

Today, the most popular DFFS model is the Define-Measure-Analyze-Design-Verify (DMADV). The DMADV model contains the first three phases of the DMAIC model. The last two phases Improve and Control are replaced by Design and Verify.

Design

Design details optimize the design and plan for design verification. This phase may require simulations.

Verify

Verify the design, set up pilot runs, implement the production process and hand it over to the process owner(s).

Statistical Thinking

Both the DMAIC and DMADV models are based on statistical thinking. The following principles form the basis for statistical thinking:

- All work occurs in a system of interconnected processes
- Inherent variation exists in all processes
- Reducing variation is the key to successfully improving a process

Recognizing Individual Tasks within the Process and Assigning Major Causes of Variability

To successfully analyze a process using statistical process control, it is important to break things down into the smallest elements possible. Accepting all processes have inherent variability and that variability can be measured. Data are used to understand variability based on the type of variability. Deming used statistical quality control techniques to identify special and common cause conditions, in which common cause was the result of systematic variability, while special cause was erratic and unpredictable.

Common Cause

Common cause variability occurs naturally in every process. Common cause variation is fluctuation caused by unknown factors resulting in a steady, but random distribution of output around the average of the data. Natural or random variation, that is inherent in a process over time, affects every outcome of the process. If a process is in-control, it has only common cause variation and can be said to be predictable. Common cause variations are due to the system itself and are somewhat expected. Examples of common cause of variability are:

- Variation in the weight of an extruded textile or plastic tubing
- Variation in moisture content of a resin
- Particle size distribution in a powder
- Poor training

Special Cause

Special cause variation is usually assigned to one of the following conditions. Variation in the process that is assignable to a specific cause or causes. For example, a variation arises because of special circumstances. Special cause variation is variation that may be assigned to a specific cause. Examples of special cause variation are:

- The first labels on a roll of self-adhesive labels are damaged, marred or otherwise unusable
- The cartons near the door of a warehouse are exposed to rain and ruined

Stabilize Processes

Traditional tools for process stabilization include process capability studies and control charts. The Six Sigma methodology supports the concept that a process may be improved by simply stabilizing the process. Making a process stable means to bring the process within the upper and lower specification limits and as close to the norm as possible.

Lean Manufacturing/Lean Thinking

Whereas the Six Sigma model concentrates on defect and mistake reduction, Lean Manufacturing and Lean Thinking (service related) concentrate on:

- Waste Reduction
- Speed
- Voice of the Customer/Employee/Business/Process

Waste Reduction

In Lean Manufacturing/Thinking other terms for waste are non-value, non-value added and the Japanese term "muda." The misconception about the term is that when items are identified as waste, it does not necessarily mean that the item will be reduced or eliminated. It simply means that it does not contribute directly to the process being studied. The reduction of waste concentrates on eight key areas: transportation, inventory, motion, waiting, over processing, over production, defects and skills.

Speed

All process improvement programs are concerned with delivering a product or service that is cost effective and has maintained a high degree of quality. Speed is also important, but not as apparent in other process improvement programs. Speed is highly recognized in Lean Manufacturing/Thinking. One avenue for speed is automation. The term automation, like the term waste, is often misunderstood. Automation simply means standardizing processes which is also a goal of Six Sigma.

Lean introduced several philosophies and tools to help in the speed and automation process to include Just-in-Time thinking principles. Individually these efforts are sometimes known as concentration of assembly, Kanban cards, bar coding, visible record systems, production leveling and work standardization.

Voice of the Customer/Employee/Business/Process

One of the unique things about the Lean methodology is an emphasis on how the customer, employee, business and process are impacted by the process improvement. These are often referred to as VOC, VOE, VOB and VOP.

ADDITIONAL METHODOLOGIES AND BODIES OF KNOWLEDGE THAT PLAY A ROLE IN LEAN SIX SIGMA

Quality Body of Knowledge (Q-BOK™) is a collection of outlines and documents maintained by the American Society of Quality (ASQ). These outlines are used for general information, reference and to study for a variety of ASQ certifications. The Q-BOK contains a Six Sigma Green Belt body of knowledge and a Black Belt Six Sigma body of knowledge. ASQ was the first to establish an industry recognized body of knowledge for Six Sigma. ASQ currently does not have a Lean Six Sigma Body of Knowledge. However, the Lean Six Sigma Body of Knowledge (SSD Global Version 3.0) contains much of the industry accepted documentation on Six Sigma.

Business Analysis Body of Knowledge (BABOK®) is maintained by the International Institute of Business Analysis. It supports six knowledge areas.

  - Business analysis planning and monitoring is concerned with which business analysis activities are needed. This includes identifying the stakeholders
  - Elicitation is obtaining requirements from the stakeholders
  - Requirements management and communication deals with contradicting requirements and changes to requirements as well as communication to stakeholders

- Enterprise analysis defines the business need and a solution scope
- Requirements analysis is the progressive elaboration of requirements into something that can be implemented
- Solution assessment and validation determines which solution is best, identifies any modifications that need to be made to the solution and an assessment of whether the solution meets the business needs

The BABOK® provides a framework that describes the areas of knowledge related to business analysis. The BABOK® is intended to describe and define business analysis as a discipline, rather than define the responsibilities of a person. The *Guide to the Business Analysis Body of Knowledge* is not really a methodology, which makes it easy to partner with Lean Six Sigma.

First published in 2005 by the International Institute of Business Analysis (IIBA), it was written to serve the project management community. The IIBA® has created the Certified Business Analysis Professional™ (CBAP®), a designation awarded to candidates who have successfully demonstrated their expertise in this field. This is done by detailing hands-on work experience in business analysis through the CBAP® application process and passing the IIBA® CBAP® examination.

Project Management Body of Knowledge (PMBOK®) is maintained by the Project Management Institute (PMI). All process improvement programs recognize that basic project management must be in place before process improvement may begin. The PMBOK® supports nine knowledge areas:

- Integration Management
- Scope Management
- Time Management
- Cost Management
- Quality Management
- Human Resource Management
- Communications Management
- Risk Management
- Procurement Management

The PMBOK® also promotes that the following phases are necessary for a successful project:

- Initiating
- Planning
- Executing

- Monitoring and Controlling
- Closing

Business Process Reengineering is an approach intended to elevate efficiency and effectiveness of an existing business process. BPR is also known as Business Process Redesign, Business Transformation and Business Process Change Management. BPR supports the following methodologies for process improvement:

- Process Identification
- Review Update As-Is State
- Design To-Be
- Test and Implement To-Be

Change Management has a variety of meanings depending on the area. All areas of change management play a role in the New Lean Six Sigma. These areas include:

- Project Management refers to a project management process where changes are formally introduced and approved
- Information Technology Service Management (ITSM) is a discipline used by IT professionals.
- People change management is a structured approach to change individuals, teams, organizations and societies

Leadership Development traditionally has focused on developing leadership ability. In a Lean Six Sigma organization, these methods are imperative to the success of Lean Six Sigma Black Belts and Master Black Belts. Successful leadership development is generally linked to the following:

- Individual's ability to learn
- Quality and nature of the leadership development program
- Genuine support for the leader's supervisor

Leaders play a key role in building a successful Lean Six Sigma organization. There are four main areas of responsibility:

- Choosing the right projects
- Choosing the right people
- Following the right methodology
- Clearly defining roles and responsibility

Measurement Systems Analysis (MSA) is a science that considers selecting the right measurement. Studying the measurement interactions along with assessing the measurement device is also part of the mix. Are measures reliable and valid? What is the measurement uncertainty?

Statistics is the science of making effective use of numerical data relating to groups of individuals or experiments. Six Sigma and Lean has always included the field of statistics when measuring and analyzing data. The *Leaner* Practitioner must make these studies more digestible for the everyday person. A stronger emphasis is placed on choosing the right software and making sure that the statistic is valid.

Business Finance plays a stronger role for *Leaner* Practitioner, the buy-in and continued support of a project cannot be based solely on statistical data. Choosing the right Return-on-Investment formula and being able to measure project success using financial terms has become essential.

As we move forward in *Leaner* practices, it is important to remember that Lean Six Sigma is not just a matter of blending two highly successful process methodologies, but rather encompassing a collection of bodies of knowledge.

Organizational Development is a body of knowledge and practice that enhances organizational performance and individual development. Today's organizations operate in a rapidly changing environment. One of the most important assets for an organization is the ability to manage change. Although there is not an industry standard established document outlining the things necessary for successful organizational development, most professionals in this field rely on the works of William Bridges. Bridges is known as one of the foremost thinkers and speakers in the areas of change management and personal transition. Themes throughout Bridges work encourage recognizing the various phases of change. The most popular being: Freezing, Changing and Re-freezing.

17

Implementation Guide

FULL-SCALE IMPLEMENTATION OF LEAN SIX SIGMA

This section is about implementing Lean Six Sigma, in the workplace, using *Leaner* as the training methodology. It is interesting to consider that other process improvement methodologies need the buy-in or approval of the department head. In the case of ISO or CMM, the effort must be endorsed by the CEO. One of the things that makes Lean Six Sigma different is that the tools and the methodology can be applied and used immediately by an individual employee. It can also be applied as a grassroots effort. Executing Lean Six Sigma basics requires no permission to get started. *Leaner* is more about the attitude and approach to projects.

There are a few basic things that will help everyone embrace *Leaner* easier. For example, it is important to remember Lean Six Sigma assumes basic project management is in place. It is essential that the team involved understands budgeting and Return-on-Investment.

Other areas of knowledge necessary to be successful in the implementation process would include Risk Management and People Management. For Risk Management this would include analysis and mitigation. For People Management this would include understanding topics such team building and project resource allocation.

Basic project management activities include:

- Planning
- Assessing Risk
- Allocation of Resources
- Acquiring Human and Non-Human Resources

Primary tools used in project management include:

- Project Charter
- Process Map
- Stakeholder's Analysis
- Responsibility and Accountability Document
- Work Breakdown Structure
- Gantt Chart
- PERT Chart

Should a Lean Six Sigma Black or Master Black Belt be planning to lead a full-scale implementation of Lean Six Sigma that includes internal certification, there is no reason why, the internal program, cannot use the same martial arts designations. Although an internal certification is not as powerful as one from an outside vendor, the advantage to internal certifications is that they can be customized.

It is also important to note, that a company can use the principles of Lean Six Sigma without building an internal training program that offers internal certification. Sometimes, learning and applying the DMAIC to projects is enough to show Return-on-Investment in process improvement efforts. Another fact to consider when building an internal program is that most employees can be trained at LSS White for Yellow Belt level. Whereas a Lean Six Sigma Green Belt is valuable to anyone trying to make their personal job better, faster or more cost effective, a company may want to limit that training to employees who will actively be participating in the process improvement effort from a cost-effectiveness point of view.

However, if the Lean Six Sigma Black or Master Black Belt see an advantage to building an internal training program, here is a quick reminder of the belts:

White Belt
Understands terminology and program goals

Yellow Belt
Understands DMAIC and tools

Green Belt
Can apply to their job or area of expertise. Tactical Responsibilities. Applies Lean Six Sigma to Specific Job

Black Belt

Strategic Responsibilities. Can Make Process Improvement in any Departments. Aligns Projects to Company Goals and Initiatives. Risk Analysis

Master Black Belt

Mentor, Coach and Teacher/Facilitator

Remember, Lean Six Sigma does not support radical change management. The science actually prefers the employee works in tandem with the existing system. The argument that best supports Lean Six Sigma implementation is that Lean Six Sigma is scalable, recognizes the importance of speed and is a quality program that is also cost effective. It does not believe that everything needs to start from the ground up or that everything needs to be changed.

Tools to express this message include:

- Voice of the Customer (VOC) Emphasis
- Collection of Data
- Analysis of Data
- Stakeholders
- Translating into Customer Requirements

To successfully implement Lean Six Sigma, it is often necessary to help people understand the concept of waste. Mistakes are usually agreed upon, but since waste or non-value is often subjective, it is useful to break out the areas of waste for discussion. These include:

- Transportation and Motion
- Over Processing/Over Production
- Defects
- Skills
- Wait Time

Using examples from the workplace when explaining these terms can be very effective. For example, discussing things such as duplication of specific reports or duplication of duties may help the concepts to resonate with the employee.

Team Building and transparency are important in applying Lean Six Sigma. Lean Six Sigma has adopted the popular paradigm that team development follows these phases:

- Forming
- Storming
- Norming
- Performing

This theory believes that successful activity in each phase is necessary to reach the next phase. This theory is also popular in other business disciplines.

To successfully implement Lean Six Sigma, much attention in detail is placed on collaboration models. These models include:

- Win/Win
- Collaboration
- Agreement
- Empathy

These strategies are also useful in negotiation and conflict management. *Leaner* additionally recognizes the following roadblocks to improvement:

- Lack of Critical Thinking
- Lack of Creative Thinking
- Lack of Basic Project Management Skills
- Poor Communication
- Lack of Motivation

Learning to recognize these conditions will give the *Leaner* Practitioner a definite advantage when dealing with change management issues.

During the implementation process, it is important to recognize the various voices mentioned throughout the body of knowledge that include:

- Voice of the Customer
- Voice of the Employee
- Voice of the Business (or Industry)
- Voice of the Process

The same tools and thinking used in the DMAIC can also be used when designing an internal Lean Six Sigma program.

To recap, in the successful implementation of an internal Lean Six Sigma program in a department or enterprise wide, the following items should be considered.

- Identification of existing processes that could be made better, faster or more cost effective. This may require assembling a steering committee with cross functional members
- Employee training in basic project management
- Employee training in the DMAIC model
- A collaborative understanding of timelines and budgets

Remember, however, any individual can always just start working in a *Leaner* way by applying the tools and the methodology of the DMAIC. The program does not have to be present to achieve amazing results.

18

Kaizen Events (Rapid Improvement Events)

Kaizen events, also known as Rapid Improvement Events, have become increasingly popular. The concept is easy to understand. Kaizen is used when a problem must be solved quickly. A team meets and swiftly determines a solution. Then just as promptly, the team, constructs a project plan or strategy. Members of the team should be comprised of Subject-Matter experts as well as those who have the authority to make and approve immediate decisions for budgets and resources.

On the manufacturing floor, Kaizen Events can often happen in real time. In the case of service or any other transactional activity, the goal of the Kaizen Event is generally to quickly produce a project plan with the budget and timeline pre-approved. In other words, the people involved in the project all agree on the direction the process improvement should take.

Many models can be used. A facilitator may be familiar with the industry or the specific process improvement or may have no knowledge of either. The facilitators job is to take the team through a structured problem-solving plan. If the problem is simple, a PDCA might work. If the issue is more complicated, the facilitator may choose a DMAIC model. There are also other Kaizen Event models that have lost popularity in favor of the DMAIC.

Regardless of the model chosen, the idea is to rapidly move through each phase of the model with the help of the facilitator. The facilitator or the project manager creates a project plan. This plan is accepted before the team disassembles.

Kaizen events should be thought of as short-duration improvement projects. Fruitful Kaizen events require pre-work. Administrative tasks, such as the securing schedules and a meeting place, are imperative to success. Participants are often coming from different locations. Also, any pre-reading and documentation that can be sent, prior to the meeting, is advisable. Kaizen events are generally 3–5 days long.

Historically, Kaizen events were performed at the C-suite level, but now it is not uncommon for Kaizen events to be conducted at mid-management or supervisory level.

The Kaizen event is basically a quality circle with cross functional members who have a stake in the process improvement being considered. Kaizen has five foundational elements:

- Teamwork
- Personal discipline
- Improved morale
- Quality circles
- Suggestions for improvement

Problems being addressed in a Kaizen meeting are issues that need to be quickly and efficiently solved. Sometimes these meetings can be intense and stressful. This is due to the pressure of determining and implementing immediate improvement. It also requires budget and resource commitments that may already be over allocated.

Kaizen is a compound word involving two Japanese concepts Kai (Change) and Zen (for the better). The term comes from Gemba Kaizen, meaning continuous improvement. The original principle promoted small-scale improvements, but in more recent times larger problems are tackled. This is partially because bringing all the main human resources together to discuss the improvement in ancillary issues related to the improvement can be costly.

Kaizen Templates are available at www.SSDGlobal.net.

Over the past few years EPA and state environmental agencies have experimented with an exciting new approach to improve government processes. Approximately 30 States and many federal agencies are using Lean and Six Sigma to achieve dramatic results. EPA, in partnership with ECOS, is working to expand the use of this continuous improvement approach. Kaizen is a popular method.

In a recent publication they found the benefits of Kaizen and Lean Six Sigma, in general, included:

- Achieved environmental results
- Ensured better customer service
- Reduced process complexity
- Enhanced process speed
- Produced quality products and services
- Improved staff morale

Popular Examples of facilitation Kaizen models include:

- PDCA
- DMAIC
- DMADV

PDCA

As a reminder, PDCA (plan–do–check–act or plan–do–check–adjust) is an iterative four-step management method used in business for the control and continuous improvement of processes and products. It is also known as the Deming circle/cycle/wheel, the Shewhart cycle, the control circle/cycle or plan–do–study–act (PDSA).

DMAIC

As a reminder, the DMAIC (an acronym for Define, Measure, Analyze, Improve and Control) (pronounced də-MAY-ick) refers to a data-driven improvement cycle used for improving, optimizing and stabilizing business processes and designs. The DMAIC improvement cycle is the core tool used to drive Six Sigma projects.

DMADV (DFSS)

DMADV, a type of Design for Six Sigma (DFSS), stands for these five phases of a Lean Six Sigma project that's aimed at creating a new product or process design: D—Define process and design goals. M—Measure (and identify) Critical-to-Quality aspects of your process/product, including risks and production capabilities. There are additional models that fall under a DFSS but DMADV is the most popular.

As a fun fact, Kaizen is a compound word involving two Japanese concepts Kai (Change) and Zen (for the better). The term comes from Gemba Kaizen, meaning continuous improvement.

The original principle promoted small-scale improvements, but in more recent times larger problems are tackled.

Free Kaizen Templates are available at http://www.SSDGlobal.net

Section VI

Additional Resources

Important Names in Lean Six Sigma

There are many contributors to Lean Six Sigma and several were the original pioneers of the Total Quality Management movement.

WALTER SHEWHART

Walter Shewhart (Shewhart) is often referred to as the "Grandfather of the quality movement." Both Edwards Deming and Joseph Juran were students of Shewhart. Dr. Shewhart believed that lack of information greatly hampered the efforts of control and management processes in a production environment. In order to aid a manager in making scientific, efficient, economical decisions, he developed Statistical Process Control methods. Walter Shewhart was the first honorary member of the American Society of Quality in 1947.

EDWARDS DEMING

The most popular name associated with quality remains Edwards Deming. Deming is credited with improving production in the United States during the Cold War, but is best known for his work in Japan. For his efforts, he was awarded the Second Order of the Sacred Treasure by the former Emperor Hirohito. Japanese scientists and engineers named the famed Deming Prize after him. It is bestowed on organizations that apply and achieve stringent quality-performance criteria. The Deming Prize is still awarded today. Two documents still referenced frequently are the Deming's 14 Points and Deming's Seven Deadly Sins. Both documents refer to conditions and thoughts about business entities in general.

JOSEPH JURAN

Joseph M. Juran helped establish the field of quality management and wrote the *Quality Control Handbook*, which taught manufacturers worldwide how to be more efficient. This book is a textbook that is still used as foundational material in most quality engineering programs. His work in quality contributed to both Six Sigma and Lean Manufacturing. He created the Pareto principle, also known as the 80–20 rule. This rules states that 80% of consequences stem from 20% of causes. Today managers use the Pareto principle to help them separate what Mr. Juran called the "vital few" resources from the "useful many."

MALCOLM BALDRIGE

Malcolm Baldrige was nominated to be Secretary of Commerce by President Ronald Reagan on December 11, 1980 and confirmed by the United States Senate on January 22, 1981. During his tenure, Baldrige played a major role in bringing quality concepts to the government. Baldrige's award-winning managerial excellence contributed to long-term improvement in economy, efficiency and effectiveness in government. Within the Commerce Department, Baldrige reduced the budget by more than 30% and administrative personnel by 25%.

The Malcolm Baldrige National Quality Improvement Act of 1987 established the Baldrige award which is given annually to companies showing the best quality approach and process improvement. Many of the basic criteria established for the award are built into the Lean Six Sigma process.

GENICHI TAGUCHI

Genichi Taguchi contributed in several areas related to Six Sigma and Lean Manufacturing primarily in the area of statistics. Three of his major contributions included the Loss Function, where he devised an equation to quantify the decline of a customer's perceived value of the product. His other major contribution was of the concept of "noise," which meant distractions could interfere with process improvement. He also created Design of Experiment screening and factorial analysis models.

ELI GOLDRATT

Eli Goldratt in Lean Six Sigma is known for his work on Theory of Constraints, which is now also called Constraint Management in the business community. The Theory of Constraints states that we know before beginning a project that constraints will be contained within the process. Goldratt gives direction and ideas on how to handle those constraints. Goldratt is also the author of a book published in the early 1990s called *The Goal*. In this book, a novel about a businessman's view of his company, Goldratt brings out many concepts such as empowerment, win-win opportunities and life balance that have been adopted philosophically by many textbooks on Lean Six Sigma.

KAORU ISHIKAWA

Kaoru Ishikawa wanted to change the way people think about work. He urged managers to resist becoming content with merely improving a product's quality, insisting that quality improvement can always go one step further. He is best known for the Ishikawa diagram, a popular fishbone chart used in process improvement and his thoughts that the job of quality belonged to everyone. This view was also supported by Joseph Juran.

Ishikawa also showed the importance of the seven quality tools: fishbone (Ishikawa diagram), control chart, run chart, histogram, scatter diagram, Pareto chart and flowchart. Additionally, Ishikawa explored the concept of quality circles.

BASIC QUALITY CONCEPTS

Leaner supports basic quality concepts such as:

- Customer Satisfaction
- Supplier Satisfaction
- Continuous Improvement

Both customer and supplier satisfaction are based on the principle of the customer or supplier feeling that process improvement is in place and not based on Return-on-Investment or other revenue factors. In all quality efforts, making things better, faster and more cost effective (continuous improvement) are the keys to success.

Summary—Core Tools Used in *Leaner* Six Sigma (L*r*SS)

This section is designed to summarize information gathered throughout this book and can be used for review purposes.

Lean Six Sigma defines process improvement as making things better, faster and more cost effective. Better is another word for quality. Quality always comes with a cost. Faster, which means more efficient, when used by the *Leaner* Practitioners, can only be achieved by eliminating or reducing a step in the process. Cost effectiveness relates to profit, savings or cost avoidance. A project that does not have the opportunity to make things better, faster or more cost effective may simply not be a process improvement project.

QUALITY IMPACT

Lean Six Sigma is a mistake-proofing program that believes prevention is always better than detection and is a primary belief in securing process improvement. Additionally, recognizing all inputs and outputs and how the inputs ultimately impact each output are constant considerations. How the inputs and outputs impact the customer is constantly assessed and reassessed. *Leaner* generally refers to Inputs as X and Outputs as Y. However, the term Key Process Input Variables (KPIVs) and Key Process Output Variables (KPOVs) are also used as well as the Vital Few Xs and the Vital Few Ys—a term used often by Joseph Juran.

There are several methods used to measure process improvement. One of the most popular being the Return-on-Investment. There are several formulas available to calculate both savings and profit. Financial terms commonly used in Lean Six Sigma are Return-on-Investment, Earned Value and Net Present Value. Many industries like to use the Balance

Scorecard technique. This technique measures improvement in the area of finance, process, training and customer impact.

Another measure especially useful when presenting an idea about quality improvement is Cost-of-Poor-Quality (COPC). In other words, what if we did not make this improvement? Would there be a ramification or penalty to pay? Industry benchmarks and metrics are also an effective way to measure both the as-is state and the actual process improvement, once it is realized.

LEAN SIX SIGMA TOOLS

The most popular tools used in Lean Six Sigma are the Seven Tools of Quality often referred to as the 7 Analytical Problem-Solving Tools or the Seven Tools of Process Improvement. Definitions of these tools are included in the *Leaner* Six Sigma Glossary available online at www.SSDGlobal.net. They include:

- Fishbone
- Flowcharting
- Check Sheets
- Histogram/Frequency Diagram
- Pareto Chart
- Scatter Diagrams
- Control Charts

Additional charts and graphs that are commonly used in Lean Six Sigma include:

- Value Stream Mapping
- Gantt
- PERT
- Swim Lane Charts
- Spaghetti Diagrams
- Tim Woods or the Eight Areas of Waste
- SWOT Analysis
- FMEA Thinking Process

Additional tools that may come in handy include

- **3 Ps**
  - People
  - Product
  - Process
- **6 Ms**
  - Machines
  - Methods
  - Materials
  - Measure
  - Mother Nature
  - Manpower
- **6 Ws**
  - What
  - Where
  - Why
  - Who
  - When
  - Which
- **8 Ds—Short for the Eight Disciplines**
  - Establish the Team
  - Describe the Problem
  - Develop an Interim Containment Plan
  - Determine Root Cause
  - Choose Corrective Action
  - Implement Action
  - Prevent Recurrence
  - Recognize the Team

THE DEFINE-MEASURE-ANALYZE-IMPROVE-CONTROL (DMAIC) MODEL

As noted earlier, Lean Six Sigma concentrates on the DMAIC model for process improvement. Here are things to consider when working with the DMAIC model also discussed in Section I.

Define

Core activities include:

- Gaining Consensus on the Statement of Work
- Completing the Project Charter
- Typical Project Charter Characteristics
  - Name/Title
  - Project Objectives
  - Scope
  - Deliverables
  - Assumptions/Constraints
  - Project ROI or Cost Savings
- Forming a Team
- Identifying the Major and Minor Stakeholders
- Key Tools in Define
- Project Charter Template
- Process Map
- Cost-Benefit Analysis
- Return-on-Investment and/or Cost Savings Calculations
- Stakeholders Analysis
- Supplier-Input-Process-Output-Customer (SIPOC) Diagram
- Critical-to-Quality (CTQ) Definitions
- DMAIC WBS
- Quality Function Deployment/House of Quality

Measure

Core activities include:

- Getting a Solid "as-is" Picture of the Current Situation
- Determining the Right Blend of Hard and Soft Metrics
- Measuring the Measurement System/Measurement Systems Analysis
- Avoiding Bias in Measurement by recognizing:
  - Linearity
  - Stability
  - Repeatability
  - Reproducibility
- Key Tools in Measure
- Detailed Process Map
- Benchmarking

- – Internal
- – Competitive
- – Functional
- – Collaborative
- – Generic
- Sigma Levels
- Return-on-Investment Calculations
- Failure Mode and Effects Analysis (FMEA)
- Industry Metrics
- Observation
- Gage R&R
- Data Collection Plans
- Scorecard

Analyze

Core activities include:

- Analyze Data
- Determine Root Causes
- Determine Correlations
- Identify Variations
- Determine Type of Data
  - – Attribute
  - – Variable
- Determine Data Characteristics
- Nominal
- Ordinal
- Interval
- Key Tools in Analyze
- Basic Statistics
- Measures of Central Tendency
  - – Mean
  - – Mode
  - – Media
- Range
- Variance
- Variation
- Correlation

- Positive
- Negative
- No Correlation
- Confidence Levels
- Confidence Intervals
  - Sample Size
  - Percentage
  - Population Size
- Advanced Statistics
- Process Capability
- Seven Tools of Quality
- The 5 Whys
- Factorial Design

Improve

Core activities include:

- List 3–5 Solutions
- Gain Consensus on a Solution
- Pilot Solution
- Rollout Solution
- Evaluate for Process Improvement
- Key Tools in Improve
- Decision Matrix /SWOT Analysis
- Narrow Down List of Solutions
- Project or Execution Plan
- Failure Mode Effects Analysis (FMEA)
- To Double Check Core Activities on Project Plan
- Evaluation Tools

Control

Core activities include:

- Verify Benefits
- Control Plan
- Transition Plan
- Key Tools in Control
- Measurement Tools
- Control Charts
- 5s Model

PRE-DMAIC TOOLS

There are several things that the *Leaner* Practitioner may elect to do prior to engaging in the DMAIC model. These include, but are not limited to:

- The Sort-Straighten-Shine-Standardize-Sustain (5s) Model
- Strengths-Weakness-Opportunity-Threats (SWOT) Model
- Plan-Do-Check-Act (PDCA) Model or Plan-Do-Study-Act (PDSA)

The 5s model is designed to physically organize an environment and consists of five phases: Sort, Straighten or Set-in-Order, Shine, Standardize and Sustain. Each phase of the model has specific steps to be followed. In Sort, the first pass, all items that are obviously bad, broken or not useful are discarded. In the Set-In-Order phase, sometimes referred to as Straighten, items are place in piles or buckets according to a pre-set criterion. For example: by colors, by seasons, by what items are used first and so forth. Shine means cleaning each pile of items, but the purpose is to identify even more items that may be discarded. Standardize is developing a system of how to handle the various piles of items that have now been designated worthy to keep. Finally, the Sustain phase, a system is developed and rolled out to keep everything in order.

A SWOT Analysis looks at quadrants to determine, via brainstorming, the Strengths, Weaknesses, Opportunities and Threats of a project. Strengths and weakness can be thought of as pros and cons. A diagram that determines the pros and cons is called a Force Field Analysis. The SWOT diagram takes on additional factors such as threats to the project or risks, as well as opportunities or possibilities. The SWOT Analysis is helpful in overall decision making.

PDCA (Plan-Do-Check-Act) and PDSA (Plan-Do-Study-Act) are two techniques aimed at promoting continuous improvement and extending a company's ability to stay ahead of a rapidly changing environment. The major difference is that "Check" is generally used to evaluate the results whereas as "Study" often is used to examine the findings.

CONSTRAINT MANAGEMENT

As discussed earlier in the bio of Eli Goldratt, the Theory of Constraints is a program to allow project managers to recognize and handle various program constraints. Goldratt addresses exploiting constraints which means making the constraint work for the individual and about developing a constraints strategy. This is also known as Constraints Management. Types of constraints are:

- Market
- Capacity
- Resources
- Suppliers
- Finance
- Knowledge or Competence
- Policy

Lean Six Sigma Green Belt Competency Model

The following criteria may be used for interview questions, testing and practical application exercises for Lean Six Sigma Green Belts.

ABILITY TO DEFINE LEAN SIX SIGMA

- Philosophy of Lean Six Sigma
- Overview of DMAIC (Define, Measure, Analyze, Improve, Control)
- Understand how Lean and Six Sigma work together

ABILITY TO EXPLAIN THE ROLES AND RESPONSIBILITIES OF LEAN SIX SIGMA PARTICIPANTS

- Master Black Belt
- Black Belt
- Green Belt
- Yellow Belt
- White Belt
- Champion
- Executive
- Coach
- Facilitator
- Team Member
- Sponsor
- Process Owner

BE ABLE TO USE THE SEVEN TOOLS OF QUALITY

- Fishbone
- Check Sheet
- Flowchart
- Histogram
- Pareto Chart
- Scatter Diagram
- Control Chart

EXPOSURE TO BASIC PROJECT MANAGEMENT

- Project Charter
- Process Mapping
- Opening and Closing a Project
- Basic Project Management Tools

DESCRIBE THE IMPACT THAT LEAN SIX SIGMA HAS ON BUSINESS OPERATIONS

- Methodologies for improvement
- Theories of Voice of the Customer (VOC), Voice of the Business (VOB), Voice of the Employee (VOE) and Voice of the Process (VOP)

ABILITY TO IDENTIFY AND EXPLAIN AREAS OF WASTE

- Excess inventory
- Space
- Test inspection
- Rework
- Transportation
- Storage
- Reducing cycle time to improve throughput
- Skills

Lean Six Sigma Black Belt Competency Model

Professional competency models are established to provide guidelines in determining expertise and knowledge in an area or subject. The following criteria may be used for interview questions, testing and practical application exercises.

ABILITY TO LEAD A DMAIC PROJECT

- Complete understanding of the Define-Measure-Analyze-Improve-Control process
- Understand leadership responsibilities in deploying a Lean Six Sigma project
- Understand change management models
- Be able to communicate ideas

ABILITY TO DESCRIBE AND IDENTIFY ORGANIZATIONAL ROADBLOCKS AND OVERCOME BARRIERS

- Lack of resources
- Management support
- Recovery techniques
- Change management techniques
- Using tools and theories such as:
  - Constraint management
  - Team formation theory
  - Team member selection

- Team launch
- Motivational management

UNDERSTAND BENCHMARKING, PERFORMANCE AND FINANCIAL MEASURES

- Best Practice
- Competitive
- Collaborative
- Scorecards
- Cost of Quality/Cost of Poor Quality (COQ/COPQ)
- Return-on-Investment (ROI)
- Net Present Value (NPV)

Use and Understand the Following Lean Six Sigma Tools

- Check Sheets
- Control Charts (also line or run charts) and be able to analyze typical control chart patterns
- Critical Path
- Fishbone
- Flowcharting
- FMEA
- Gantt Chart
- Histogram
- Pareto Chart
- PERT Chart
- Scatter Diagrams
- Spaghetti Diagrams
- Swim Lane Charts
- SWOT Analysis
- Tim Woods or the Eight Areas of Waste
- Value Stream Mapping (Basic)

Understand These Core Concepts

- Understand Various Types of Benchmarking: Competitive, Functional, Collaborative and Internal

- Define Business Performance Measures such as Key Performance Indicators (KPIs)
- Construct Scorecards including Balance Scorecards
- Comprehend Financial Measures such as: Use the rest of that sentence starting with Revenue Growth and ending with Cost-Benefit Analysis
- Define and Distinguish between Various Types of Benchmarking, Including Best Practices, Competitive and Collaborative
- Define Various Business Performance Measures, Including Balanced Scorecard, Key Performance Indicators (KPIs) and the Financial Impact of Customer Loyalty
- Define Financial Measures, such as: Revenue Growth, Market Share, Margin, Cost of Quality (COQ)/Cost of Poor Quality (COPQ), Net Present Value (NPV), Return-on-Investment (ROI) and Cost-Benefit Analysis

Leaner supports the concept that all process improvement programs are rooted in Total Quality Management (TQM) concepts and that process improvement first begins with a firm understanding of Project Management basics as outlined in the Project Management Body of Knowledge (PMBOK®). Lean Six Sigma Black Belts and Master Black Belts should be well versed in these areas.

Leaner further supports that the newer and *Leaner*, Lean Six Sigma, which is based on Six Sigma with a heavy emphasis in Lean Manufacturing/Lean Thinking has evolved to include other established bodies of knowledge. In addition to basic TQM and the PMBOK®, successful Lean Six Sigma Black Belts and Master Black Belts should review, study and monitor these additional bodies of knowledge:

- Business Analysis Body of Knowledge (BABOK®)
- Business Process Reengineering (BPR)
- Change Management
- Leadership Development
- Measurement Systems Analysis
- Statistics
- Business Finance
- Organizational Development

Lean Six Sigma Master Black Belt Competency Model

Professional competency models are established to provide guidelines in determining expertise and knowledge in an area or subject. The following criteria may be used for interview questions, testing and practical application exercises.

ABILITY TO IDENTIFY AND LEAD A DMAIC PROJECT

- Ability to teach and facilitate the Define-Measure-Analyze-Improve-Control process
- Demonstrate leadership in deploying a Lean Six Sigma project
- Deploy and monitor change management models
- Superior verbal and written presentation skills

ABILITY TO CREATIVELY DEAL WITH ROADBLOCKS AND OVERCOME BARRIERS RELATED TO

- Lack of resources
- Management support
- Recovery techniques
- Change management techniques

TEACHING AND MENTORING KNOWLEDGE OF TOOLS AND THEORIES TO INCLUDE

- Constraint management
- Team formation theory
- Team member selection
- Team launch
- Motivational management

PREPARE, EXPLAIN AND EVALUATE FACTORS RELATED TO BENCHMARKING, PERFORMANCE AND FINANCIAL MEASURES

- Best Practice
- Competitive
- Collaborative
- Scorecards
- Cost of Quality/Cost of Poor Quality (COQ/COPQ)
- Return-on-Investment (ROI)
- Net Present Value (NPV)

USE, EVALUATE AND EXPLAIN

- Check Sheets
- Control Charts (also line or run charts) and be able to analyze typical control chart patterns
- Critical Path
- Fishbone
- Flowcharting
- FMEA
- Gantt Chart
- Histogram
- Pareto Chart

- PERT Chart
- Scatter Diagrams
- Spaghetti Diagrams
- Swim Lane Charts
- SWOT Analysis
- Tim Woods or the Eight Areas of Waste
- Value Stream Mapping (Basic)

DEVELOP, DELIVERY, EVALUATE TRAINING PLANS

- Design training plans
- Understand various training approaches
- Build curriculum
- Demonstrate success
- Ability to coach and mentor Black, Green and Yellow Belts

ADDITIONAL DESIGN CRITERIA

- Business Performance Measures such as
- Balanced Scorecard
- Key Performance Indicators (KPIs)
- Financial measures
  - Revenue Growth
  - Market Share
  - Margin
  - Cost of Quality (COQ)/Cost of Poor Quality (COPQ)
  - Net Present Value (NPV)
  - Return-on-Investment (ROI)
  - Cost-Benefit Analysis

Note: *Leaner* supports the concept that all process improvement pro-grams are rooted in Total Quality Management (TQM) concepts and that process improvement first begins with a firm understanding of Project

Management basics as outlined in the PMBOK®. Master Black Belts should be well versed in areas covered in these evolving documents. It is also suggested that Master Black Belts familiarize themselves with ISO 13053, ISO 12500 and PRINCE2® and keep updated on new releases associated with these documents.

Lean Six Sigma Key Terms

4M's: four word categories used to provoke thought on an Ishikawa diagram (cause and effect diagram). Material, Method, Machine, Man.

5 Whys: the practice of asking why five times when presented with a problem to try to identify potential root causes.

5S: a process and method for creating and maintaining an organized, clean, safe and high-performing workplace. The steps are Sort, Set, Shine, Standardize and Sustain.

A3 report: a Toyota developed standard report showing a problem, analysis and corrective action plan on a single piece of paper usually A3 size.

A-B control: a method used to regulate working relationships between a pair of operations such that overproduction is minimized. Machine A cannot feed machine B until it is empty or waiting for work.

ABC production analysis: volume-based groupings used to segment part numbers in order to define the inventory policy that they fall within.

abscissa: the horizontal axis of a graph.

acceptance criteria: these are specific criteria identified by the customer for each functional requirement. The acceptance criteria are written in simple terms and from a perspective of the customer.

acceptance region: the region of values for which the null hypothesis is accepted.

acceptance testing: acceptance testing is a validation activity conducted to determine whether a system satisfies its acceptance criteria. It is the last phase of the software testing process.

affinity diagram: organizes brainstorming ideas into categories or themes. Useful when there are large amounts of information collected during a brainstorming session. It is also called the KJ method, after Kawakita Jiro (a Japanese anthropologist) who first developed the idea.

agile: a conceptual framework for undertaking software projects. Agile methods are not a single approach.

alpha risk: the probability of accepting the alternate hypothesis when the null hypothesis is true.

alternative hypothesis: a tentative explanation which indicates that an event does not follow a chance distribution, a contrast to the null hypothesis.

andon: the Japanese word for "signal" referring to a visual system that provides an indicator to supervision when abnormalities occur within processes.

ANOVA: analysis of variance—this is a statistical test done by comparing the variances around the means of the condition being compared. In the simplest form, ANOVA gives a statistical test of whether the means of several groups are all equal.

ANOVA Gage R&R: measures the amount of variability induced in measure by the measurement system itself and compares it to the total variability observed to determine the viability of the measurement system.

assemble to order: an environment where a product or service can be assembled or provided upon receipt of a customer's order. The product will usually consist of several modules that are assembled to the highest level possible and stored such that when the order arrives, it can be assembled quickly and to the customer's specification.

assignable cause: a source of variation which is non-random, a change in the source ("Vital Few" variables) will produce a significant change of some magnitude in the response (dependent variable). For example, a correlation exists, the change may be due to an intermittent in-phase effect or a constant cause system which may or may not be highly predictable, an assignable cause is often signaled by an excessive number of data points outside limits, an unnatural source of variation, most often economical to eliminate.

assignable variation: variation in data which can be attributed to specific causes.

assumption: there may be external circumstances or events that must occur for the project to be successful (or that should happen to increase your chances of success). If you believe that the probability of the event occurring is acceptable, you could list it as an assumption. An assumption has a probability between 0% and 100%. That is, it is not impossible that the event will occur (0%) and it is not a fact (100%). It is somewhere in between. Assumptions are important because they set the context in which the entire remainder of the project is defined. If an assumption doesn't come through, the estimate and the rest of the project definition may no longer be valid.

attribute: a characteristic that may take on only one value, for example or 1.

attribute data: numerical information at the nominal level, subdivision is not conceptually meaningful, data which represents the frequency of occurrence within some discrete category, For example, 42 solder shorts.

automatic line stop: ensuring that processes producing will stop whenever a defect or problem occurs.

autonomation: a term developed by Taiichi Ohno to describe "automation with human touch." Autonomated machine will stop when abnormalities occur so that they will not create large amounts of scrap and do not need an operator to watch the machine.

average: also called the "mean," it is the arithmetic average of all the sample value. It is calculated by adding all the sample values together and dividing by the number of elements(n) in the sample.

background variables: variables that are of no experimental interest and are not held constant. Their effects are often assumed insignificant or negligible or they are randomized to ensure that contamination of the primary response does not occur.

balance chart: a bar chart or histogram that illustrates work content per operator. Can be used to balance work for operators or machines in order to achieve improvements in flow.

balanced scorecard: is a performance management approach that focuses on customer perspective, internal business processes and learning and growth and financials. It was originated by Drs. Robert Kaplan (Harvard Business School) and David Norton as a performance measurement framework that added strategic non-financial performance measures to traditional financial metrics to give managers and executives a more "balanced" view of organizational performance.

batch and queue: typical mass production method such that a part going through a system will be produced in large batches to maximize "efficiency" and then sit in a queue waiting for the next operation.

benchmarking: a standard used to compare performance against best-in-class companies. It then uses the information gathered to improve its own performance. Subjects that can be benchmarked include strategies, products, programs, services, operations, processes and procedures.

beta risk: the probability of accepting the null hypothesis when the alternate hypothesis is true.

blocking variables: a relatively homogenous set of conditions within which different conditions of the primary variables are compared. Used to ensure that background variables do not contaminate the evaluation of primary variable.

bottleneck: a bottleneck is a sort of congestion in a system that occurs when workload arrives at a given point more quickly than that point can handle it. It is metaphorically derived from the flowing of water through a narrow-mouthed bottle where the flow of water is constrained by the size of its neck.

breakthrough improvement: a rate of improvement at or near 70% over baseline performance of the as-is process characteristics.

brownfield: a brownfield site is an existing facility that is usually managed in line with mass production methods.

bugs: a software bug is a problem causing a program to crash or produce invalid output. It is caused by insufficient or erroneous logic and can be an error, mistake, defect or fault.

build to order: a production environment when a product or service can be made and assembled after receipt of a customer's order.

Burndown chart: a burndown chart is a visual tool for measuring and displaying progress. Visually, a burndown chart is simply a line chart representing remaining work over time. Burndown charts are used to measure the progress of an agile project at both an iteration and project level.

capability: measurement index that expresses the capability of the process by suing a percentage. Or even simpler, the ability to do something.

capital linearity: a philosophy linked to capital expenditure on machinery such that a small amount of additional capacity can be added by using several smaller machines rather than one big and very expensive machine.

casualty: the principle that every change implies the operation of a cause.

causative: effective as a cause.

cause: that which produces an effect or brings about change.

cause and effect diagram: also called a fishbone diagram. This is a graph that places the issue being discussed in the head of the fish. The bones of the fish are categories of problems that could be a problem. The smaller bones are the possible root causes.

cell: a cell is a group of people, machines, materials and methods arranged so that processing steps are located adjacent to each other and in sequential order. This allows parts to be processed one at a time or, in some cases, in a constant small batch that is maintained through the process sequence. The purpose of a cell is to achieve and maintain an efficient, continuous flow of work.

center line: the line on a statistical process control chart which represents the characteristic's central tendency.

central tendency: data clustered around the middle. Mean, mode and median are all examples of central tendency.

chaku-chaku: one-piece flow ideal whereby machines automatically unload parts so that an operator can move apart from one machine to the next without stopping to unload parts.

champion: a person who supports the successful completion of the project.

characteristic: a process input or output which can be measured and monitored.

classification: differentiation of variables.

client/customers: the person or group that is the direct beneficiary of a project or service is the client/customer. These are the people for whom the project is being undertaken (indirect beneficiaries are stakeholders). In many organizations, internal beneficiaries are called "clients" and external beneficiaries are called "customers," but this is not a hard and fast rule.

common cause: see Random Cause.

common causes of variation: sources of variability in a process which are truly random. These are generally inherent in the process itself and can be managed. This type of variation is a usual, historical, quantifiable variation in a system.

complexity: the level of difficulty to build, solve or understand something based on the number of inputs, interactions and uncertainty involved.

confidence level: the probability that a random variable x lies within a defined interval.

confidence limits: the two values that define the confidence level.

confounding: allowing two or more variables to vary together so that it is impossible to separate their unique effects.

constraints: constraints are limitations that are outside the control of the project team and need to be managed around.

consumer risk: probability of accepting a lot when, in fact, the lot should have been rejected (see Beta Risk).

continuous data: a set of observations usually associated with physical measurement that can take on any mathematical value within specified parameters. Or more simply put, the sequencing of activities.

continuous flow: each process, whether in an office or plant setting, makes or completes only the one piece that the next process needs, the batch size is one. Single-piece flow or one-piece flow, is the opposite of a batch-and-queue process.

continuous random variable: a random variable which can assume any value continuously in some specified variable.

control chart: the most powerful tool of statistical process control. It consists of a run chart, together with statistically determined upper and lower control limits and a centerline.

control limits: upper and lower bounds in a control chart that are determined by the process itself. They can be used to detect special or common causes of variation.

control specifications: specifications called for by the product being manufactured.

cost of poor quality (COPQ): the costs associated with any activity that is not doing the right thing right the first time.

critical path: the series of consecutive activities that represent the longest time path through the process. The critical path is the sequence of activities that must be completed on schedule for the entire project to be completed on schedule. It is the longest duration path through the work plan. If an activity on the critical path is delayed by 1 day, the entire project will be delayed by 1 day (unless another activity on the critical path can be accelerated by 1 day).

critical-to-quality (CTQ): any activity or thought related to the successful outcomes of the project.

cross dock: a facility that gathers and recombines a variety of inbound materials and parts from multiple suppliers to forward on to multiple customers.

cutoff point: the point which partitions the acceptance region from the reject region.

cycle efficiency (CE): CE is a measure of the relative efficiency in a production system. It represents the percentage of value-added time of a product through the critical path vs. the total cycle time (TCT).

cycle time: this is the time a person needs to complete an assigned task or activity before starting again.

cycle time interval: the frequency that an item is made during a set period of time (usually days).

daily standup/Scrum: a daily standup is a whole team meeting that happens at the same time every day that usually lasts 15 minutes or less. Each team member should provide the following information: What did I do yesterday, what am I planning to do today and what impediments do I currently have?

data: information used as a basis for reasoning, discussion or calculation, often refers to quantitative information.

defect: an output of a process that does not meet a defined specification, requirement or desire such as time, length, color, finish, quantity or temperature.

defective: a unit of product or service that contains at least one defect.

degrees of freedom: the number of independent measurements available for estimating a population parameter.

deliverable: a deliverable is any tangible outcome that is produced by the project. All projects create deliverables. These can be documents, plans, computer systems or building blueprints. Internal deliverables are produced because of executing the project and are usually needed only by the project team. External deliverables are those that are created for clients and stakeholders. Your project may create one or many deliverables.

demand: the usage of an item over a period. This also includes an understanding of the customer requirements for quality, lead time and price.

density function: the function which yields the probability that a random variable takes on any one of its possible values.

dependent variable: a response variable, for example, y is the dependent or "Response" variable where Y=f (XI…Xn) variable.

design of experiments (DOE): an efficient, structured and proven approach to interrogating a process or system for the purpose of maximizing the gain in process or system knowledge.

design for Six Sigma (DFSS): the use of Six Sigma thinking, tools and methods applied to the design of products. Any Six Sigma model for managing a project, that is not DMAIC, is generally considered a DFSS.

distributions: tendency of large numbers of observations to group themselves around some central value with a certain amount of variation or "scatter" on either side.

DMAIC: this acronym stands for "Define, Measure, Analyze, Improve and Control." It is the heart of the Six Sigma process and refers to a data-driven quality strategy for improving processes. It is an integral part of any company's Six Sigma quality initiatives.

done: also referred to as "Done-Done," this term is used to describe all the various tasks that need to happen before a story is considered potentially releasable.

DPMO: the total number of defects detected in some number of units divided by the total number of those units.

effect: that which was produced by a cause.

engineer to order: products whose customer's specifications are unique for each order, therefore each product is engineered from scratch upon receipt of an order.

epic: a very large user story that is eventually broken down into smaller stories.

estimation: the process of agreeing on a size measurement for the stories, as well as the tasks required to implement those stories in a product backlog.

exits: the amount of work completed over a given amount of time measured in £s or units.

experiment: a test under defined conditions to determine an unknown effect, to illustrate or verify a known law, test or establish a hypothesis.

experimental error: variation in observation made under identical test conditions. Also called residual error. The amount of variation which cannot be the variables included in the experiment.

factors: independent variables.

failure mode and effects analysis (FMEA): a procedure used to identify, assess and mitigate risks associated with potential product, system or process failure modes.

feature creep: feature creep occurs when a software becomes complicated and difficult to use as a result of too many features.

FIFO: a strategically sized inventory that keeps the sequence of the production uniform throughout the value Stream maintaining flow.

fishbone diagram: See cause and effect diagram.

fixed-effects model: experimental treatments are specifically selected by the researcher. Conclusion only applies to the factor levels considered in the analysis. Inferences are restricted to the experimental levels.

fixed-position stop system: a problem addressing method on continuously moving production lines such that if a problem is identified and not resolved before a fixed point, the production line will stop.

flowchart: a graphic model of the flow of activities, material and/or information that occurs during a process.

fluctuations: variances in data which are caused by many minute variations or differences.

frequency distribution: the pattern or shape formed by the group of measurements in a distribution.

Gage R&R: is used in Measurement Systems Analysis (MSA) quantitative assessment of how much variation (repeatability and reproducibility) is in a measurement system compared to the total variation of the process or system.

Gantt chart: a Gantt chart is a bar chart that depicts activities as blocks over time. The beginning and end of the block correspond to the beginning and end-date of the activity.

gemba: Japanese term used to describe the "actual place" where value is added or the shop floor.

greenfield: a new production facility not restricted by practices of the past, therefore having a culture of adapting change without resistance.

heijunka: leveling the production by product and/or quantity over a fixed time period.

high-level value stream map: a visual representation of the aggregated material and information flows within a company or business unit.

histogram: a bar chart that depicts the frequencies (by the height of the plotted bars) of numerical or measurement categories.

homogeneity of variance: the variances of the groups being contrasted are equal (as defined by statistical test of significant differences).

hoshin: the Japanese word for planning and used throughout operational, financial, strategic and project-based scenarios.

independent variable: a controlled variable, a variable whose value is independent of the value of another variable.

input: a resource consumed, utilized or added to a process or system. Synonymous with X, characteristic and input variable.

inspection: mass production would use inspectors outside of a process. Lean producers assign the responsibility of quality to the areas where the processes are performed. Inspections are performed within the areas that own the assembly process.

instability: unnaturally large fluctuations in a pattern.

interaction: the combined effect of two factors observed over and above the singular effect of each factor against the level of the other factor. A significant interaction indicates that the effect of each factor on the response changes depending on the value of the other factor.

interval: numeric categories with equal units of measure, but no absolute zero point, that is quality scale or index.

inventory turns: a measure to quantify the pace at which inventory rotates throughout a company. Inventory turns = annual cost of goods sold/average value of inventory during year.

jidoka: quality built into processes such that if a process is not capable of creating the required output, then it will not operate until it can.

jishuken: a Japanese word used to describe a "hands-on learning workshop."

just in time (JIT): stands for "just in time." This means producing or conveying only the items that are needed by the next process when they are needed and in the quantity needed. This process can even be used between facilities or companies.

kaikaku: radical improvement designed to quickly eliminate and/or add value to a value stream. Also described as "Breakthrough Kaizen."

Kaizen: incremental change for the better. The organized use of common sense to improve cost, quality, delivery, safety and responsiveness to customer needs.

Kaizen event: a rapid improvement event, part of a continuous improvement program. A focused, dedicated and well-defined event that is used to get quick hit value by implementing "do-now" solutions leading to waste elimination.

Kanban: Kanban, pronounced /'kan'ban/, is a method for developing products with an emphasis on just-in-time delivery and the optimization of flow of work on the team. It emphasizes that developers pull work from a queue and the process, from definition of a task to its delivery to the customer, is displayed for participants to see.

Kanban post: a storage container for Kanban cards pulling deliveries.

labor linearity: a manning philosophy such that as demand increases or reduces, manpower is added one at a time as such manpower requirements are linear to production volume.

lead time: the total time from the beginning of the supply chain to the time something needs to ship. The sum of the VA/NVA time for a product to move through the entire value stream.

Lean: a method used to create more value for customers by identifying and eliminating non-value activities

Lean transactional: the application of Lean to business processes such as paperwork flow through an office in accounts or marketing.

level selling: the eliminating of sales spikes generated by end of month sales targets at dealers and so forth. This allows for improved flow of demand from the customer and improvements in anticipated demand.

lifecycle: refers to the process used to build the deliverables produced by the project. There are many models for a project lifecycle.

line charts: charts used to track the performance without relationship to process capability of control limits.

linear regression: analyzes the relationship between two variables, X and Y.

long-term variation: the observed variation of an input or output characteristic which has had the opportunity to be observed over time.

lower control limit (LCL): used in control charts to show the lower limit. Typically, three standard deviations below the central tendency.

machine cycle time: the amount of time unit spends in the operational cycle of a machine.

mean: the statistical measure on a sample that is used as an estimate of the mean of the population from which the sample was drawn. Numerically equals the sum of scores divided by the number of samples.

measurement accuracy: for a repeated measurement, it is a comparison of the average of the measurements compared to some known standard.

measurement precision: for a repeated measurement, it is the amount of variation that exists in the measured values.

median: the middle value of a data set when the values are arranged in either ascending or descending order.

metric: a measure that is a key indicator of performance. It should be linked to goals or objectives and carefully monitored.

milestone: a milestone is a scheduling event that signifies the completion of a major deliverable or a set of related deliverables. A milestone, by definition, has duration of zero and no effort. There is no work associated with a milestone. It is a flag in the work plan to signify that some other work has completed. Usually, a milestone is used as a project checkpoint to validate how the project is progressing. In many cases there is a decision, such as validating that the project is ready to proceed further, that needs to be made at a milestone.

milk run: reducing transport costs and batch sizes by performing multiple pick up and drops at multiple suppliers using one truck.

mixed-effects model: contain elements of both the fixed- and random-effects models.

muda: the Japanese word for waste or Non-Value-Added Activity.

mura: the Japanese word used to describe variation or fluctuation.

muri: the Japanese word used to describe overburdening or strain/stress.

nemawashi: a Japanese expression used to describe the practice of obtaining support and buy-in for change by firstly the idea and then the plan with upper management and stakeholders. Directly translated means "preparing" the ground for planting.

nominal: a type of data used to label variables without providing any quantitative value. Nominal data cannot be ordered and cannot be measured.

non-conforming unit: a unit which does not conform to one or more specifications, standards and/or requirements.

non-conformity: a condition within a unit which does not conform to some specific specification, standard and/or requirement, often referred to as a defect, any given non-conforming unit can have the potential for more than one non-conformity.

non-value added (NVA): any activity performed in producing a product or delivering a service that does not add value.

normal distribution: the distribution characterized by the smooth, bell-shaped curve.

null hypothesis: a tentative explanation which indicated that a chance distribution is operating, a contrast to the null hypothesis.

obeya: translated as "Big Room," this is the expression used by the Japanese to describe the powerful project room concept also known as a "war room."

objective: an objective is a concrete statement that describes what the project is trying to achieve. The objective should be written at a low level, so that it can be evaluated at the conclusion of a project to see whether it was achieved. Project success is determined based on whether the project objectives were achieved. A technique for writing an objective is to make sure it is Specific, Measurable, Attainable/Achievable, Realistic and Time bound (SMART).

one piece flow: making and moving only one piece or part at a time. See Continuous Flow.

one-sided alternative: the value of a parameter which has an upper bound and a lower bound, but not both.

operator cycle time: the time it takes an operator to go through all his or her work elements before repeating them.

order interval: represents the frequency (days) that a part is ordered.

ordinal: ordered categories (ranking) with no information about distance between each category, that is rank ordering of several measurements of an output parameter.

ordinate: the vertical axis of a graph.

over production: the process of producing more, sooner or faster than is required by the next process or customer.

P charts: charts used to plot percent defectives in a sample.

pacemaker: the only point in the production process that is scheduled and therefore dictates the pace of production for a whole system of processes.

pacesetter: the point in the process that limits the output of the total process.

parameter: a constant defining a particular property of the density function of a variable.

Pareto diagram: a chart which ranks or places in order, common occurrences.

perturbation: a non-random disturbance.

pitch: the amount of time required by a production area to make one container of products. Takt time x pack-out qty=pitch.

plan for every part (PFEP): a comprehensive plan for each part consumed within a production process. This would take the form of a spreadsheet or simple table and contain such data as pack-out quantity, location of use and storage and order frequency. This provides one accurate source of information relating to parts.

plan, do, check, act (PDCA): an improvement cycle introduction to the Japanese in the 1950s by W. Edwards Deming. Based upon proposing then implementing an improvement, then measuring the results and acting accordingly.

Poka-yoke: mistake-proof device or procedure designed to prevent a defect from occurring throughout the system or process.

population: a group of similar items from which a sample is drawn. Often referred to as the universe.

power of an experiment: the probability of rejecting the null hypothesis when it is false and accepting the alternative hypothesis when it is true.

prevention: the practice of eliminating unwanted variations of priori (before the fact), for example, predicting a future condition from a control chart and when applying corrective action before the predicted event transpires.

primary control variables: the major independent variables in the experiment.

probability: the chance of something happening in percent or number of occurrences over many trials.

probability of an event: the number of successful events divided by the total numbers of trials.

problem: a deviation from a specified standard.

problem solving: a process of solving problems, the isolation and control of those conditions which generate or facilitate the creation of undesirable symptoms.

process: a method of doing something, generally involving several steps or operations.

process average: the central tendency of a given process characteristics across a given amount of time or a specific point in time.

process control chart: any of several various types of graphs upon which data are plotted against specific control limits.

process control: see statistical process control.

process owner: has responsibility for process performance and resources. They provide support, resources and functional expertise to Six Sigma projects. They are accountable for implementing developed Six Sigma solutions into their process.

process spread: the range of values in which a given process characteristic displays, this term most often applies to the range, but may also encompass the variance. The spread may be based on a set of data collected at a specific point in time or may reflect the variability across a given amount of time.

producer's risk: probability of rejecting a lot when, in fact, the lot should have been accepted (see Alpha Risk).

product backlog: acts as a repository for requirements targeted for release at some point. These are typically high-level requirements with high-level estimates provided by the product stakeholders. The requirements are listed on the backlog in priority order and maintained by the product owner.

product owner: the product owner represents the voice of the customer and is accountable for ensuring that the team delivers value to the business. The Product Owner writes customer-centric items (typically user stories), prioritizes them and adds them to the product backlog. Scrum teams should have one Product Owner.

production Kanban: a signal that specifies the type and quantity of product that an upstream process must produce.

program: a program is the umbrella structure established to manage a series of related projects. The program does not produce any project deliverables. The project teams produce them all. The purpose of the program is to provide overall direction and guidance, to make sure the related projects are communicating effectively, to provide a central point of contact and focus for the client and the project teams and to determine how individual projects should be defined to ensure that all the work gets completed successfully.

program manager: a program manager is the person with the authority to manage a program. (Note that this is a role. The program manager may also be responsible for one or more of the projects within the program.).

project: a project is a temporary structure to organize and manage work and ultimately to build a specific defined deliverable or set of deliverables. All projects are unique, which is one reason it is difficult to compare different projects to one another.

project definition (charter): before you start a project, it is important to know the overall objectives of the project, as well as the scope, deliverables, risks, assumptions and be familiar with the project organization chart.

project phase: a phase is a major logical grouping of work on a project. It also represents the completion of a major deliverable or set of related deliverables.

project team: the project team consists of the full-time and part-time resources assigned to work on the deliverables of the project. They are responsible for understanding the work to be completed, completing assigned work within the budget, timeline and quality expectations.

pull: material flow triggered by actual customer need rather than a scheduled production forecast. Downstream process signal to upstream processes exactly what is required and in what quantity.

push: the production of goods regardless of demands or downstream need, usually in large batches to ensure "efficiency."

quality function deployment (QFD): a systematic process used to integrate customer requirements into every aspect of the design and delivery of products and services. Output graphic is often the House of Quality.

R charts: plot of the difference between the highest and lowest in a sample Range Control Chart.

random: selecting a sample so each item in the population has an equal chance of being selected, lack of predictability.

random cause: a source of variation which is random, a change in the source ("trivial many"). For example, a correlation does not exist, any individual source of variation results in a small amount of variation in the response, cannot be economically eliminated from a process, an inherent natural source of variations.

random-effects model: experimental treatments are a random sample from a larger population of treatments. Conclusion can be extended to the population. Interferences are not restricted to the experimental levels.

random sample: one or more samples randomly selected from the universe (population).

random variable: a variable which can assume any value of a set of possible values.

random variations: variations in data which result from causes which cannot be pinpointed or controlled.

randomness: a condition in which any individual event in a set of events has the same mathematical probability of occurrences as all other events within the specified set, that is, individual events are not predictable even though they may collectively belong to definable distribution.

range: the difference between the highest and lowest in a set of values or "subgroup."

ranks: values assigned to items in a sample to determine their relative occurrence in a population.

ratio: numeric scale which has an absolute zero point and equal units of measure through, that is measurements of an output parameter, that is amps.

regression analysis: includes any techniques for modeling and analyzing several variables. Linear regression was the first type of regression analysis to be studied rigorously and to be used extensively in practical applications.

reject region: the region of values of which the alternate hypothesis is accepted.

repeatability (of a measurement): the extent to which repeated measurements of an object with a particular instrument produce the same value.

replication: observations made under identical test conditions.

representative sample: a sample which accurately reflects a specific condition or set of conditions within the universe.

reproducibility (of a measurement): the extent to which repeated measurements of an object with a particular individual produce the same value.

requirements: requirements are descriptions of how a product or service should act, appear or perform. Requirements generally refer to the features and functions of the deliverables you are building on your project. Requirements are a part of project scope. High-level scope is defined in your project definition (charter). The requirements form the detailed scope. After your requirements are approved, they can be changed through the scope change management process.

research: critical and exhaustive investigation or experimentation having for its aim the revision of accepted conclusion in the light of newly discovered facts.

residual error: See Experimental Error.

response time: the time that an order needs to be satisfied.

retrospective: a team meeting that happens at the end of every iteration to review lessons learned and to discuss how the team can be more efficient in the future. It is based on the principles of applying the learning from the previous sprint to the upcoming sprint.

rework: activity required to correct defects produced by a process.

risk: there may be potential external events that will have a negative impact on your project if they occur. Risk refers to the combination of the probability the event will occur and the impact on the project if the event occurs. If the combination of the probability of the occurrence and the impact to the project is too high, you should identify the potential event as a risk and put a proactive plan in place to manage the risk.

robust: the conditions or state in which a response parameter exhibits hermetic to external cause of a non-random nature, that is impervious to perturbing influence.

safety stock: inventory held to compensate for variation in demand, quality and downtime.

sample: one or more observations drawn from a larger collection of observations or universe (population).

scatter diagrams: charts which allow the study of correlation. For example, the relationship between two variables.

scope: scope is the way you describe the boundaries of the project. It defines what the project will deliver and what it will not deliver. High-level scope is set in your project definition (charter) and includes all your deliverables and the boundaries of your project. The detailed scope is identified through your business requirements. Any changes to your project deliverables, boundaries or requirements would require approval through scope change management.

scope change management: the purpose of scope change management is to manage change that occurs to previously approved scope statements and requirements. Scope is defined and approved in the scope section of the project definition (charter) and the more detailed business requirements. If the scope or the business requirements change during the project (and usually this means that the client wants additional items), the estimates for cost, effort and duration may no longer be valid.

Scrum: Scrum is a framework within which people can address complex adaptive problems, while productively and creatively delivering products of the highest possible value. It is based on the adaptive and iterative methodology.

Scrumban: Scrumban is a mix between Scrum and Kanban, which supposedly contains the best features of both methods.

Scrum master: Scrum is accountable for removing impediments to the ability of the team to deliver the sprint goal/deliverables. The Scrum Master is not the team leader, but acts as a buffer between the team and any distracting influences. The Scrum Master ensures that the Scrum process is used as intended. The Scrum Master is the enforcer of rules. A key part of the Scrum Master's role is to protect the team and keep them focused on the tasks at hand. The role has also been referred to as servant-leader to reinforce these dual perspectives.

sensei: Japanese word for "teacher" and denotes mastery within their field of knowledge. A Sensei should be a wise and easily understood mentor that guides thinking with his subjects rather than dictates the point to promote learning.

setup time: the amount of time required to changeover a process after producing the last part of one product to the first good part of the next product.

short-term variation: the amount of variation observed in a characteristic which has not had the opportunity to experience all the sources of variation from the inputs acting on it.

signal Kanban: a signal that triggers an upstream process to produce, when a minimum quantity is reached at the downstream process.

single minute exchange of die (SMED): a technique to reduce setup or changeover times to eliminate the need to build in batches.

spaghetti chart: a visual chart showing the path taken by a product or person during a process to highlight excessive motion.

special cause: see Assignable cause.

special cause variation: non-random causes of variation.

specification limits: the boundaries of acceptable performance.

spike: a short, time-boxed piece of research, usually technical, on a single story that is intended to provide just enough information that the team can estimate the size of the story.

sponsor (executive sponsor and project sponsor): the sponsor is the person who has ultimate authority over the project. The executive sponsor provides project funding, resolves issues and scope changes, approves major deliverables and provides high-level direction. He or she also champions the project within the organization. Depending on the project and the organizational level of the executive sponsor, he or she may delegate day-to-day tactical management to a project sponsor. If assigned, the project sponsor represents the executive sponsor on a day-to-day basis and makes most of the decisions requiring sponsor approval. If the decision is large enough, the project sponsor will take it to the executive sponsor.

sprint/iteration: a fixed duration period where user stories are chosen to work on. The term Sprint comes from the Scrum methodology and is analogous to the term Iteration. A sprint is defined as a 2–4-week period.

sprint backlog: at the beginning of each sprint, the team has sprint planning with a result being a backlog of work that the team anticipates completing at the end of the sprint. These are the items that the team will deliver against throughout the duration of the sprint.

sprint planning: is a pre-sprint planning meeting attended by the core agile team. During the meeting, the Product Owner describes the highest priority features to the team as described on the product backlog. The team then agrees on the number of features they can accomplish in the sprint and plans out the tasks required to achieve delivery of those features. The planning group works the features into User Stories and assigns Acceptance criteria to each story.

sprint review: each Sprint is followed by a Sprint review. During this review the software developed in the previous Sprint is reviewed and if necessary new backlog items are added.

stable process: a process which is free of assignable causes, for example, in statistical control.

stakeholder: specific people or groups who have a stake in the outcome of the project are stakeholders. Normally stakeholders are from within the company and may include internal clients, management, employees and administrators. A project can also have external stakeholders, including suppliers, investors, community groups and government organizations.

standard deviation: one of the most common measures of variability in a data set or in a population. It is the square root of the variance.

standardized work: a defined work method that describes the proper workstation and tools, work required, quality, standard inventory knacks and sequence of operations.

statistical control: a quantitative condition which describes a process that is free of assignable/special causes of variation, for example, variation in the central tendency and variance. Such a condition is most often evidence on a control chart, that is, a control chart which displays an absence of non-random variation.

statistical process control (SPC): use of basic graphical and statistical methods for measuring, analyzing and controlling the variation of a process for the purpose of continuously improving the process.

steering committee: a steering committee is usually a group of high-level stakeholders who are responsible for providing guidance on overall strategic direction. They don't take the place of a sponsor, but help spread the strategic input and buy-in to a larger portion of the organization. The steering committee is especially valuable if your project has an impact in multiple organizations because it allows input from those organizations into decisions that affect them.

story points: unit of estimation measuring complexity and size.

subgroup: a logical grouping of objects or events which displays only random event-to-event variations, for example, the objects or events are grouped to create homogenous groups free of assignable or special causes. By virtue of the minimum within group variability, any change in the central tendency or variance of the universe will be reflected in the "subgroup-to-subgroup" variability.

supermarket: a strategically controlled store of parts used by downstream processes.

supplier: vendor or entity responsible for providing an input to a process in the form of resources or information.

symptom: that which serves as evidence of something not seen.

system: that which is connected according to a scheme.

systematic variables: a pattern which displays predictable tendencies.

takt time: rate of demand from customer. It is the available operating time for the requirement. Or more simply put, the availability service time divided by the customer demand rate Takt time enables your organization to balance the pace of its service outputs to match the rate of the customer demand.

task: a user story can be broken down into one or more tasks. Tasks are estimated daily in hours (or story points) remaining by the developer working on them.

task board/storyboard: a wall chart with cards and sticky notes that represents all the work for each sprint. The notes are moved across the board to show progress.

team: the Team is responsible for delivering the product. A Team is typically made up of 5 to 9 people with cross-functional skills who do the actual work (analyze, design, develop, test or technical communications). It is recommended that the "Team" be self-organizing and self-led, but still work with some form of project or team management.

test of significance: a procedure to determine whether a quantity subjected to random variation differs from postulated value by an amount greater than that due to random variation alone.

theory: a plausible or scientifically acceptable general principle offered to explain phenomena.

theory of constraints: theory describes the methods used to maximize operating income when an organization is faced with bottleneck operations. This theory also deals with how to handle the unknown.

time boxing: time boxing is a planning technique common in planning projects where the schedule is divided into several separate time periods (time boxes, normally 2 to 6 weeks long), with each part having its own deliverables, deadline and budget.

total cycle time (TCT): the time taken from work order release into value stream until completion/movement of product into shipping/finished goods.

total productive maintenance: a means of maximizing production system efficiency by analyzing and eliminating down-time through up-front maintenance.

Toyota production system: the production system developed and used by the Toyota Motor Company which focuses on the elimination of waste throughout the value stream.

trend: a gradual, systematic change over time or some other variable.

two-sided alternative: the value of a parameter which designates an upper and lower bound.

type I error: see Alpha Risk.

type II error: see Beta Risk.

unnatural pattern: any pattern in which a significant number of the measurement do not group themselves around a center line, when the pattern is unnatural it means that outside disturbances are present and are affecting the process.

upper control limit: a horizontal line on a control chart (usually dotted) which represents the upper limits of process capability.

user persona: personas are a description of the typical users of a given software. A persona description should include: skills, background and goals.

user story: a user story is a very high-level definition of a requirement, containing just enough information so that the developers can produce a reasonable estimate of the effort to implement it. A user story is a brief description explaining the intention in simple language that capture what the users want to achieve. A user story is also a placeholder for conversation between the users and the team.

value: this term refers to a product or service capability that is provided to a customer at the right time and at an appropriate price.

value-added activity: any activity that changes the product in terms of fit, form or function toward something that a customer is willing to pay for.

value-added time: the time expanded in value-added activity to produce a unit. Time for those work elements that transform the product in a way for which the customer is willing to pay for.

value stream: all activities, both value-added and non-value added, that are required to bring a product, group or service from the point of order to the hands of a customer and a design from concept to launch to production to delivery.

value stream map: a visual representation of a process showing flow of information and material through all steps from the supplier to the customer.

variable: a characteristic that may take on different values.

variables data: numerical measurement made at the interval or ratio level, quantitative data, for example, ohms, voltage, diameter, subdivision of the measure scale are conceptually meaningful, for example, 1.6478 volts.

variation: any quantifiable difference between individual measurements, such differences can be classified as being due to common causes (random) or special causes (assignable).

variation research: procedures, techniques and methods used to isolate one type of variation from another (for example, separating product variation from test variation).

velocity: it is a relative number which describes how much work the team can get done over a period.

visualization: the design of a workplace such that problems and issues can be identified without timely and in-depth investigation. Truly visual workplaces should be capable of assessment in less than 3 seconds.

VOB: the voice of the business is derived from financial information and data. Voice of the business: Represents the needs of the business and the key stakeholders of the business. It is usually items such as profitability, revenue, growth and market share.

VOC: voice of the customer—Represents the expressed and non-expressed needs, wants and desires of the recipient of a process output, a product or a service. It is usually expressed as specifications, requirements or expectations.

VOE: voice of the employee. Represents the expressed and non-expressed needs, wants and desires of what the employee needs to be successful.

VOP: voice of the process—Represents the performance and capability of a process to achieve both business and customer needs.

waste (muda): includes anything that does not add value to a final product or service, an activity that consumes valuable resources without creating customer value.

WIP (work in process): these are items—material or information—that are between machines, processes or activities waiting to be processed, any inventory between raw materials and finished goods.

withdrawal Kanban: a signal that specifies the type and quantity of product that the downstream process may withdraw.

work cells: an arrangement of people, machines, materials and methods such that processing steps are adjacent and in sequential order.

work plan (schedule): the project work plan tells you how you will complete the project. It describes the activities required, the sequence of the work, who is assigned to the work, an estimate of how much effort is required, when the work is due and other information of interest.

X&R charts: a control chart which is a representation of process capability over time, displays a variability in the process average and range across time.

Index

Note: Page numbers in *italic* refer to figures, respectively.